CERTIFICATION PREP

Adobe Photoshop Creative Cloud

Common
Occupational
Readiness
Essentials

by

D. Michael Ploor, MBA
National Board Certified Teacher
STEM Curriculum Integration Specialist
School District of Hillsborough County
Tampa, Florida

Publisher
The Goodheart-Willcox Company, Inc.
Tinley Park, Illinois
www.g-w.com

Cover image: MrGarry/Shutterstock.com

Table of Contents

Introduction

The Common Occupational Readiness Essentials (CORE) series of certification preparation guides focuses on mastering the essential basic skills needed as a workplace-ready user of the software. The goal of each CORE certification preparation guide is to provide practice in each essential basic skill required by employers who use the software. To prove workplace readiness, you will also be prepared to take the official certification exam for the software.

CORE Adobe Photoshop Creative Cloud will help prepare you to take the Adobe Certified Associate (ACA) Adobe Photoshop Creative Cloud certification exam. It provides step-by-step instruction for the features and commands covered on the certification exam. The focus of the lessons is to practice *using* the actual commands and features instead of creating a complete end product. Most lesson content is created using the software, and minimal downloading of files is required. Furthermore, each certification preparation guide is broken down into small learning units to enable better comprehension and application of the software. Where required, answers are provided at the back of the certification preparation guide.

Certification as an Adobe Certified Associate demonstrates an aptitude with Adobe software. ACA certification is offered for Adobe Dreamweaver, Adobe Flash, Adobe Photoshop, Adobe Premier, Adobe Illustrator, and Adobe InDesign. Certification exams are provided by Certiport, Inc., through various testing facilities. Visit www.certiport.com for more information on registering for certification exams.

About the Author

D. Michael Ploor is the author of the CORE series of certification preparation guides. Mr. Ploor's students have achieved exceptional results with the CORE certification preparation guides. His students collectively pass more than 500 industry certification exams each year without the need for other preparation materials. Mr. Ploor has demonstrated the strength of integrating the CORE guides in a diverse mix of courses.

Mr. Ploor is also the author of three textbooks on the subject of video game design: *Introduction to Video Game Design, Video Game Design Foundations,* and *Video Game Design Composition.* He is a National Board Certified Teacher in Career and Technical Education and holds an MBA degree from the University of South Florida. He maintains professional teaching credentials in Business Education and Education Media Specialist.

Mr. Ploor is at the forefront of innovative teaching and curriculum. He developed STEM curriculum while serving as the lead teacher in the Career Academy of Computer Game Design at Middleton Magnet STEM High School. Mr. Ploor has applied his skills as a STEM Curriculum Integration Specialist in designing innovative curriculum and by collaborating to construct the state standards for video game design in several states. He has also been instrumental in authoring competitive events for Career and Technical Student Organizations such as the Future Business Leaders of America (FBLA) and Phi Beta Lambda (PBL).

In addition to publishing textbooks and lessons, Mr. Ploor provides professional development as a frequent presenter at regional and national conferences to promote CTE education and video game design curriculum.

Lesson 1
Elements of Art and Principles of Design

Objectives

Students will compare and contrast traditional artwork and digital artwork. Students will describe the seven elements of art. Students will apply the principles of design.

Introduction to Traditional and Digital Artwork

Artwork is an artistic work developed using a combination of art elements to create a visual scene, character, volume, or image. *Traditional artwork* is created without the use of computer technology. Examples of traditional artwork include paintings, drawings, sculptures, pottery, and so on. *Digital artwork* is created using a computer. The artist inputs information into a computer program that helps create the artwork. The final artwork can be displayed in physical form or in virtual form. Digital artwork can be output in physical form such as a printed page or an object produced by molding, rapid prototyping machine, computer-guided lathe, or other computer-controlled output. Digital artwork in virtual form may be digital pictures or animations displayed on a computer screen.

Whether the artist is working with virtual media like a video game or physical media like a sculpture, the elements of art and principles of design hold true. Thousands of years of trial and error by artists have established these universal truths.

The *elements of art* deal with the individual features needed to compose artwork. Each individual feature or element is constructed and arranged to create artwork. Artwork should also be developed following the principles of design. The *principles of design* govern how to effectively combine the elements of art to compose a pleasing work of art.

Elements of Art

There are seven elements of art: shape, form, line, color, value, space, and texture. Each of these elements details an aspect of a single attribute of an object. These elements are universal and apply to both traditional and digital art. Below are brief descriptions of each element of art.

Shape

The black circle shown in **Figure 1-1** is a shape defined by the edges of the black ink on the paper. Shape is a defined area in two-dimensional space. Shapes come in two different varieties: geometric and organic.

Geometric shapes are regular figures, like a square, circle, triangle, octagon, or trapezoid. Geometric shapes are also known as 2D primitives. *Primitives* are regular shapes and objects that are used to assemble more complex shapes or objects. For example, the robotic character shown in **Figure 1-1** is constructed from 2D primitives: three circles, five rectangles, and one trapezoid.

Irregular shapes are known as *organic shapes.* Organic shapes describe things like a cloud, tree, blowing steam, or even an ergonomic computer mouse. Mostly, organic shapes are used to describe things in nature. In practice, organic shapes describe natural and unnatural shapes that have curved or irregular edges.

Form

The assembly of 2D shapes to represent a third dimension is *form.* Form shows measurable dimensions of length, width, and depth for an object. A traditional sculpture has form, but a computer-modeled character also has form.

Line

If you look at the basic robot in **Figure 1-1,** each shape is defined by the boundary created by a solid black line. A line is the path between two points and is most often used as a boundary to create a shape. Lines can be straight, curved, looping, or organic and can be solid or composed of dashes or other marks.

When a line is composed of dashes or other marks, it is an implied line, as shown in **Figure 1-2.** An *implied line* is the path the viewer's eye takes to connect the two endpoints of the line when it is not continuous. Basically, the viewer's eye connects the dots with an invisible (implied) line to complete the line path.

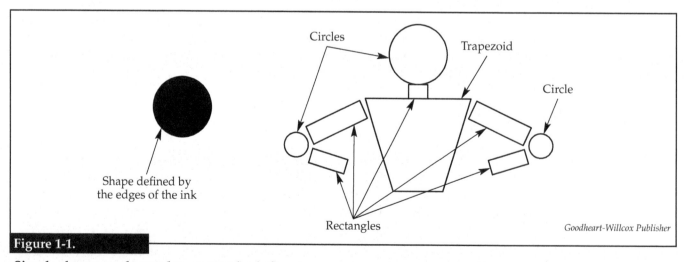

Goodheart-Willcox Publisher

Figure 1-1.

Simple shapes can be used to create a basic figure.

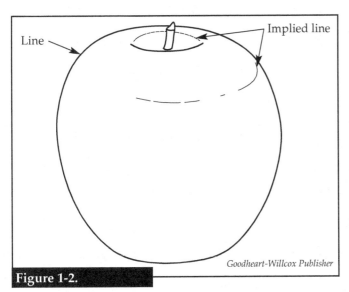

Figure 1-2.

Both lines and implied lines are used to compose this apple.

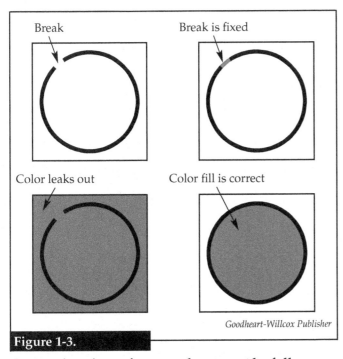

Figure 1-3.

In most imaging software, a shape must be fully enclosed by a line in order to be filled.

Color

The combination of hues applied to a line or shape is its color. *Hue* is the pure color. Hue can be tinted or shaded to add additional colors. A *tint* is a hue with white added. A *shade* is a hue with black added. Tinted colors are lighter and shaded colors are darker than the hue. A *tone* is a hue with both black and white, or gray, added.

In imaging software, the *line color* or *outline color* is applied to the border line only. The *shape color* or *shape fill* is color applied to the shape defined by the line. In most imaging software, the shape color can be applied only if the shape is completely enclosed by lines or the edges of other shapes. If there is a break in the line or the shape is not completely enclosed, the color will "leak out," as shown in **Figure 1-3.**

A color wheel illustrates the relationship of primary, secondary, and tertiary colors, as shown in **Figure 1-4.** *Primary colors* are red, yellow, and blue. All other colors are created from the three primary colors. *Secondary colors* are created by blending two primary colors. *Tertiary colors* are created by blending a primary and a secondary color or two secondary colors. *Analogous* colors appear adjacent to each other on the color wheel. Red, orange, and yellow are analogous colors, and they appear in a group on the same side of the color wheel. *Complementary* colors are opposite each other on the color wheel. Complementary colors create high contrast. Purple is a complementary color to yellow. Yellow text will be easily seen if it is placed on a purple background.

Value

Value is the use of light and dark to add highlight, shading, or shadows. If you look at a *monochromatic* image, which is an image with one hue, the entire image is created based on the principle of value. Look at the image of the apple shown in **Figure 1-5.** By using just the black hue, the image can have shape, line, and value. Value of the black hue is shades of gray. Depth is created around the stem of the apple by darkening that area. Near the top of the apple, depth is created by lightening the part of the apple that is closest to the light.

All objects shown on a computer screen are composed of pixels, or picture elements. *Pixels* are the smallest areas of illumination on an electronic display. In digital artwork, artists use pixel shading to add to the illusion of depth. *Pixel shading* is the use of lighter and darker colors, or changes in value, to create light and shadow. As objects get farther from the light source, the objects are darkened so they appear farther from the source.

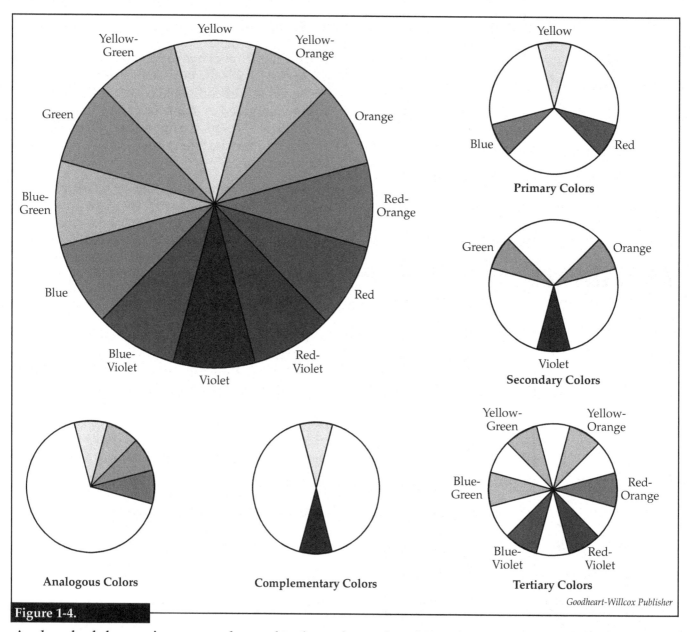

Goodheart-Willcox Publisher

Figure 1-4.

A color wheel shows primary, secondary, and tertiary colors and can be used to identify analogous and complementary colors. Refer to the color wheel image file on the student companion website.

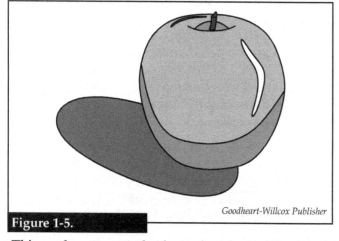

Goodheart-Willcox Publisher

Figure 1-5.

This apple was created using only values of black.

Space

The area or volume in a scene is the space. Space may be physical or virtual. A sculpture occupies physical space. An artist actually cuts into the block of marble and creates a statue with physical length, width, and depth. However, using a computer, an artist can create in virtual space. The object created in a 3D modeling program has virtual length, width, and depth. In 2D art, whether physical or virtual, space must be represented with illusion.

Positive and negative space apply emphasis to the design. *Positive space* is the area or volume occupied by the primary objects. *Negative space* is the area or volume around or between the primary objects. An example of these can be found in a portrait photograph. You are the positive space. The volume between you and the background is the negative space. The amount of negative space in a design can help provide contrast and emphasis to the primary objects. Imagine the portrait is taken as a panoramic view in a stadium. While you are still a primary object, you are surrounded by hundreds of other objects. You are hard to identify as the primary object in the photograph. This is because there is little negative space to separate you from everything else. Without any negative space, your image has less emphasis than it did in the portrait of just you in front of a background. A scene can become cluttered if there is not enough negative space.

In three-dimensional space, length, width, and depth dimensions are used to create an object. When working with a 2D surface like a sheet of paper or a computer screen, the artist must trick the eye to create the illusion of 3D space. In computer rendering, artists apply both pixel shading and vertex shading to help create the illusion of 3D. *Vertex shading* is moving the points on an object to resize it such that the object appears smaller in the distance. The principle of visual perspective is applied during vertex shading.

Visual perspective is the proportional scaling of objects as they move toward a vanishing point. In **Figure 1-6,** notice how the parallel lines of the path angle inward until the lines meet in the distance. Of course, the sides of the path remain parallel. It is just the principle of visual perspective that makes the sides of the path appear to converge. Also, notice how the tree trunks appear to get thinner in the distance. Each object is scaled down as it moves toward the vanishing point. The point where receding parallel lines appear to meet is the *vanishing point.* There may be one, two, or three vanishing points, but one- and two-point perspectives are the most common. A two-point perspective is shown in the drawing in **Figure 1-6.**

Also notice in **Figure 1-6** that the trees closest to the viewer appear to be in focus, while the trees in the distance appear out of focus. This effect can be applied in artwork to help enhance the illusion of depth. By adding a blur effect to an object in the distance, the spatial relationship of near or distant objects is enhanced. The spatial relationship describes how an object appears in space in relation to the viewer.

Texture

Variations in form and color create texture, which is an uneven surface. *Tactile texture* is an irregular surface that can be physically felt, like sandpaper. When you touch it, you feel the surface is bumpy or rough. This texture is a variation in surface depth to create a coarse physical sensation. *Optical texture* is creating variation in what you see. The skin of an orange has an optical texture because the color changes around the orange. The surface of the orange is not a single solid color. Additionally, the orange has tactile texture because the surface has physical bumps that can be felt.

Principles of Design

The principles of design are the set of rules or guidelines used to create artwork. The principles of design are specific to make sure you are creating effective layouts or art. Depending on the type of design (web, game, fine art, or other), the number

Anson0618/Shutterstock.com

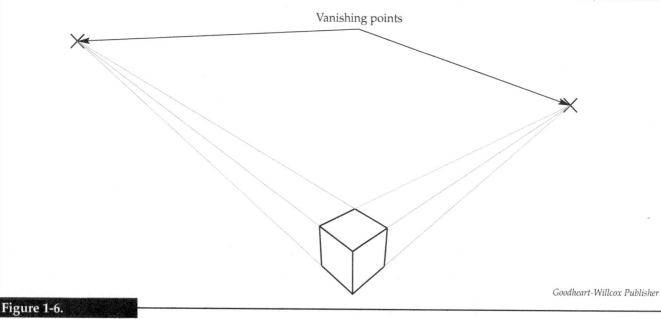

Vanishing points

Goodheart-Willcox Publisher

Figure 1-6.

The edges of the path and the rows of trees appear to converge at a single vanishing point.

of principles will change. For most digital design projects, the principles of design are movement, emphasis, harmony, variety, balance, contrast, proportion, pattern, and unity.

Movement

Applied action is *movement*. In traditional art forms, a static picture must convey movement. Often in digital art, movement is done through animation. However, an

Figure 1-7.

Even though this image is not moving, movement is communicated.

Clipart.com

artist must understand and apply the movement principle even if the object is going to be animated.

Look at **Figure 1-7** and see how movement is represented in the illustration. The tassels on the jacket are drawn to the right instead of straight down. This implies the snowboarder is moving to the left. Additionally, bits of snow are drawn to the right of the snowboarder, which also imply movement to the left. Lines are added to imply movement. Straight lines imply the leftward movement, while curved lines imply the legs and outstretched arm are moving. Finally, the position of the snowboarder implies movement. For the snowboarder to be in that pose, it is logical to interpret movement, and the fact that the character is looking to the left implies leftward movement.

Emphasis

When a designer draws attention to an object, the object is given *emphasis.* Emphasis can be achieved by making an object larger, brighter, repeated, or moving. The idea behind adding emphasis is that the viewer will understand the object is special in some way in relation to other objects in the scene.

Harmony

Using similar elements is the principle of *harmony.* Harmony helps hold the image or scene together. Imagine a dirty character dressed in old raggedy clothes, but wearing a gold crown. The gold crown just does not fit with the way the character is dressed. The design of this character is not demonstrating harmony. Likewise, the elements of a scene need to have harmony. Objects that are out of place, such as a cell phone in a scene of an 18th century café, detract from the experience of the viewer.

Variety

The purposeful absence of harmony to create visual or contextual interest is the principle of *variety* (also known as alternation). This differs from emphasis in that the design is less obvious. It takes keen observations or thinking by the viewer to discover the cue. Without variety, artwork may be boring and lacking visual interest.

Balance

Objects arranged such that no one section overpowers any other part is called *balance.* When constructing a work of art, the artist needs to divide the canvas into equal parts to measure balance. Balance can be established as either symmetrical or asymmetrical, as shown in **Figure 1-8.**

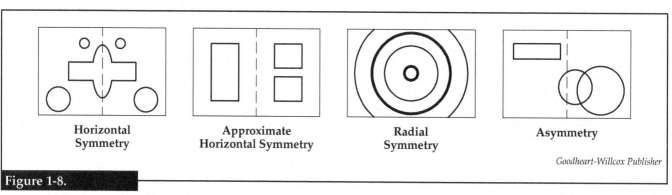

Horizontal Symmetry   Approximate Horizontal Symmetry   Radial Symmetry   Asymmetry

Goodheart-Willcox Publisher

Figure 1-8.

Symmetry and asymmetry can be used in graphic design.

Symmetrical Balance

When the right and left sides, top and bottom, or all sides are equal, *symmetrical balance,* or formal balance, is created. If the image is split down the middle, both halves contain the same number and size of objects. An example of symmetrical balance is your eyes on your face. Your nose is in the center, and one eye on each side of your nose provides symmetrical balance. Since the right side of your face is a mirror image of the left side, this is called *horizontal symmetry.* Symmetry can also be established from a center point and radiate equally from that center. *Radial symmetry* is equal in length from a center point. An example of radial symmetry is the rings created by dropping a pebble into a puddle.

Asymmetrical Balance

Asymmetrical balance, or informal balance, is the use of similar objects to create balance, or the use of color and light balance instead of object balance. Unlike symmetrical balance in which the right and left sides may be mirror images, asymmetrical balance can be seen in something like a bookshelf. The shelves balance the amount of space taken up by the books, but the size, shape, color, and arrangement of the books differs on each shelf. The concept is that a lot of something small can balance a little of something big. A swarm of small bees provides asymmetrical balance to a single large beehive. This can work with color as well, where a small area of a vibrant color provides asymmetrical balance to a large area of a neutral color.

Asymmetrical balance is often confused with asymmetry. *Asymmetry* means that the work is not at all balanced. Placing objects off-center or heavy to one side of a work can draw the viewer to an area of attention, as shown in **Figure 1-8.**

Proximity

The final element of balance is proximity. *Proximity* is how closely objects are arranged. In a social setting, placing characters close to each other conveys a meaning such as friendship or family. Conversely, placing characters far apart conveys a meaning such as enemy, stranger, or rival. Proximity can help create tension. Placing an object such as a stick of dynamite near an open fire creates tension as these two elements will cause an explosion if combined. Proximity can also help show scale or relative size. Placing a character next to a doorway provides scale to the height of the character.

Rule of Thirds

The rule of thirds can be used to help achieve balance. The *rule of thirds* is a guideline that states an image should be divided into three sections horizontally and three sections vertically to create nine areas. This is like putting a tic-tac-toe board on top of the image. Where the lines cross are the focal points for a scene. Placing the objects you want the viewer to focus on at these points will draw the viewer's eye to those objects.

Contrast

The variation of color and brightness to make objects stand out from each other is *contrast.* Imagine placing blue text on a blue background. The viewer would not be able to read the letters. The designer needs to select a color, such as yellow or orange, that contrasts with the blue background. Alternately, the brightness of the blue used for either the text or background can be varied to provide contrast. Light blue text on a dark blue background may provide enough contrast for the viewer to read the words. This same principle applies to objects. Imagine using a red ball on a red background. The ball needs to contrast with the background to be seen easily.

Proportion

Proportion is the size of an object in relation to the other objects around it. Proportion may be exaggerated to make something more noticeable or prominent or reduced to make it more subtle. To create a realistic scene, the designer will try to show objects in proper proportion to the other objects in the scene as much as possible.

Proportion is also used to give the illusion of depth, or a third dimension. The concept of visual perspective states that an object looks smaller in the distance and gets larger as it approaches the viewer. In the Renaissance period of art, the concept of trompe l'oeil was applied to art. *Trompe l'oeil* translates to "fool the eye." Art of this type uses perspective, depth, and shadow to create ultrarealistic scenes. **Figure 1-9** shows the ceiling of the Jesuitenkirche (Jesuit church) in Vienna, Austria. The artist has made it appear as if there is a dome, but the dome does not exist. A painting of the trompe l'oeil type appears to the viewer as if looking out of a window at a real landscape or object.

Pattern

When an element is repeated, a *pattern* is created. Patterns occur in both visual layout and in motion. Visually, pattern is applied in one of three ways: regular, flowing, and progressive.

Paolo Gianti/Shutterstock.com

Figure 1-9.

The dome in this photograph does not exist. It is a painting created to fool the viewer's eye.

Figure 1-10.

This static two-dimensional image communicates not only movement, but depth.

A regular pattern has repeating objects of similar size and spacing, such as seen on a checkerboard. Flowing patterns have more organic shapes than regular patterns and mimic movement, as shown in **Figure 1-10.** A simple example of flowing pattern is an arrow or curve that leads to a point. The eye follows the curve from the thickest end to the point, which provides a feeling of movement or motion. Progressive patterns display a sequence or series of steps. This is a visual pattern used in animations. In static (not animated) art, a progressive pattern can simulate continuing motion or progression within a single frame, such as the image shown in **Figure 1-10.**

In animations, such as on websites, objects move in patterns. For example, if the animation is of a character running across the top of a web page as a background image scrolls, the artist must balance the pace of the animation with the movement of the background. If these are not synchronized, the animation will appear odd to the viewer.

Unity

All of the elements and principles of art work together to create unity. When something has *unity*, it appears as a single piece and not an assembly of different parts. The easiest way to explain this is to look at a character, such as Indiana Jones. The Indy character has a hat, whip, leather jacket, over-the-shoulder bag, fedora, dungarees, and boots. Each of these pieces is one part of the whole. When these pieces come together, a single character is created that has a sense of unity.

Unity also applies to the layout of a scene. Each component of the scene should look like it fits with the others. Many times, the unity of the entire project is overlooked. For example, on a multipage website the designer should strive for *site-wide consistency.* The color, layout, and location of buttons should be the same on each page. Imagine how frustrating it would be if the Home button were in a different place on each page of the website. Also, colors should be maintained to increase consistency. By adding unity elements to each page, the site feels like a single document. Without unity, the user may feel like he or she is jumping from one website to another.

Maintaining unity in the graphic design of a game, website, or user interface has the benefits of shorter development time, easier maintenance, and improved usability. Using the same items such as navigation buttons will shorten development time by not having to design new buttons for every page or level. Using copy and paste to add the same button to a different page is much faster than creating a new button. This also ensures the button is exactly the same on each page. Maintenance is also simplified by having the same items on each page. When making a change to a user interface button, the designer would only need to upload one new image file and all the buttons referencing that file would be updated. Users also benefit from the reuse of buttons through improved usability of the website or user interface. The user would quickly learn the location of buttons and how the user interface works. Each new page or level would feel familiar. This adds to the user's understanding and navigation of the program. As an added benefit, reusing the same buttons or objects also reduces the overall file size and provides faster loading and shorter download times.

Lesson Review

Vocabulary

In a word processing document or on a sheet of paper, list all of the *key terms* in this lesson. Place each term on a separate line. Then, write a definition for each term using your own words. You will continue to build this terminology dictionary throughout this certification guide.

Review Questions

Answer the following questions. These questions are aligned to questions in the certification exam. Answering these questions will help prepare you to take the exam.

1. List the seven elements of art.

   _____

   _____

2. What are primitives?

   _____

   _____

3. From which colors are all colors on the color wheel created?

   _____

   _____

4. What is the difference between a complementary and an analogous color?

   _____

   _____

5. What is the difference between positive space and negative space?

   _____

   _____

   _____

   _____

6. What is a vanishing point?

_____

_____

_____

_____

7. List the principles of design for most design projects.

_____

_____

8. Which principle of design involves implied action for an object?

_____

9. Which principle of design involves drawing attention to an object by making it brighter, larger, or moving?

_____

10. Which principle of design is demonstrated by the images below?

_____

Pixel Embargo/Shutterstock.com   kaband/Shutterstock.com

11. Describe how the rule of thirds helps alignment of elements in a scene or image.

_____

_____

_____

_____

12. Which principle of design describes why a blue object is hard to see on a blue background?

_____

13. Which principle of design involves making all the parts of a scene work together?

_____

14. Why would a designer copy and paste the same button design on all web pages on a website?

_____

15. What are three benefits of maintaining unity of design?

_____

_____

_____

_____

Lesson 2
Color Models, Images, and Fonts

Objectives

Students will describe common color models. Students will classify images as raster or vector. Students will discuss sizing and resolution of digital images. Students will identify serif and sans serif fonts.

Color Models

Colors are defined using a *color model*, which is a way of mixing base colors to create a spectrum of colors. The RGB and CMYK color models are the most common color models used in graphic design. The name of the *RGB* color model comes from the three base colors used in the color model: red, green, and blue. All of the colors you see on a computer screen are made by mixing these three base colors. The name of the *CMYK* color model comes from the process colors used in commercial printing: cyan, magenta, and yellow. K stands for key color. The most detail in a printed image appears in the key color, which is almost always black. Other color models include hue, saturation, luminescence (HSL); hexadecimal; and L*A*B* color, as shown in **Figure 2-1.**

The *hue, saturation, and luminescence (HSL)* color model, also known as the hue, saturation, and brightness (HSB) color model, creates color by adjusting these elements. Hue is the pigment color, saturation is how dark or rich the color is, and luminescence or brightness is how much light is shining on the color. This model is popular in creating textures and surfaces for 3D models. Since 3D models require the use of light and shadow to define position relative to the light source, using this color model allows the computer to leave the hue and saturation of the texture unchanged while adjusting the luminescence setting to be brighter on the surface facing the light source and darker on the surface facing away from the light source.

Hexadecimal color model is an RGB color model in which colors are represented by a series of six letters and numbers. This color model is used in web page design.

Color Model	Features	Method
HSL (also known as HSB or HSV)	Creates color by a combination of hue, saturation, and luminescence (or brightness or value). This model is popular in creating textures and surfaces for 3D models. Since 3D models require the use of light and shadow to define position relative to the light source in the game, using this color model allows the computer to leave the hue and saturation of the texture unchanged while adjusting the luminescence setting to be brighter on the surface facing the light source and darker on the surface facing away from the light source.	Additive
RGB	Creates color by a combination of red, green, and blue. Blending these three colors allows for over 16 million colors at 8-bit depth.	Additive
RGBA	The RGB color model with support for alpha channels. Alpha channels are transparency channels. The alpha channel sets the saturation of an RGB color from full opacity (not see-through) to full transparency (completely see-through).	Additive
Hexadecimal	An RGB color model in which the color is represented as a series of six letters and numbers. This color model is used in web page design. Many imaging software programs allow the user to limit colors to "web only," which are 216 colors universally compatible with web browsers.	Additive
CMYK	Creates color by a combination of cyan, magenta, yellow, and a key color that is almost always black. This model is used for printed materials. Each of the colors corresponds to one of the four printing plates on a printing press.	Subtractive
L*A*B*	The description of the L*A*B* color model is a bit complicated as the L is for lightness and the A and B components are derived from a nonlinear color matrix, similar to an X,Y coordinate graph. This model seeks to create natural-looking colors. Additionally, L*A*B* color model is used to convert RGB color models to CMYK color models or vice versa. L*A*B* color works for both video displays (RGB) and printed materials (CMYK) and is considered device independent.	Matrix of both additive and subtractive combinations

Goodheart-Willcox Publisher

Figure 2-1.

A comparison of common color models.

Many imaging software programs allow the user to limit colors to "web only," which are 216 colors universally compatible with web browsers.

The *L*A*B** color model seeks to create natural colors as the human eye would see them. The description of the L*A*B* color model is a bit complicated as the L is for lightness and the A and B components are derived from a nonlinear color matrix, similar to an X,Y coordinate graph. Additionally, L*A*B* color model is used to convert RGB color models to CMYK color models or vice versa. L*A*B* color works for both video displays (RGB) and printed materials (CMYK) and is considered device independent.

The total spectrum of colors a given model can create is called the *gamut.* Colors are assembled or blended using an additive or subtractive method. The *additive method* starts with no color, or black, and colors are added to create the final color. White in an additive color model is the combination of all color wavelengths in light. In the RGB color model, black is red 0, green 0, and blue 0. This means no color is added to the black screen. White is red 255, green 255, and blue 255. This means the maximum amount of all three colors is added to the black screen.

The *subtractive method* starts with all color, or white, and colors are removed to create the final color. For example, when you look at a red object, all color wavelengths in the light are absorbed by the paint (subtracted) except for red. What you see is the red wavelength. White is the reflection of all color wavelengths, so no color is subtracted. Black occurs when no color wavelengths are reflected, so all color is subtracted. CMYK is a subtractive color model. Black is cyan 100%, magenta 100%, yellow 100%, and key 100%. White is cyan 0%, magenta 0%, yellow 0%, and key 0%.

Images

There are two basic types of images: raster and vector. All images created using a computer fall into one of these two categories. Additionally, digital images may be compressed to save storage space and reduce transmission times.

Raster Images

Raster images are images that are made of dots or pixels. Each pixel in the image has a specific color and location to construct the final image. A raster image is called a *bitmap* because the location and color of each pixel is mapped. The computer reads a bitmap image by creating a coordinate grid with the origin at the top-left corner and increasing the X value moving right and the Y value moving down. In each space of the coordinate grid is a single pixel. A pixel can only be one color. To determine the color of a pixel at a particular coordinate location, the color value of a pixel is read by the computer and displayed.

Originally, bitmaps were only made at a bit depth of 1. **Bit depth** is a binary measurement for color. Binary allows for only two values, either a 1 or a 0. A bit depth of 1 describes the exponent value of the binary digit. A bit depth of 1 means 2^1. A bitmap value of 1 would, therefore, assign a white pixel on the coordinate grid where required. This produces a black and white image with no gray.

Eventually, computers were able to read bitmaps to a bit depth of 4. A bit depth of 4 allowed for a total of 16 colors, as 2^4 equals 16. The modern minimum standard for computer-displayed color is a bit depth of 8 or higher. A bit depth of 8, or 2^8, allows for 256 colors. Two hundred fifty-six–color devices are typically handheld devices where graphic quality is not needed. Computer monitors, HDTVs, and other devices that require quality graphics try to achieve true color or deep color.

True color has a bit depth of 24. True color uses the familiar RGB color model with 256 shades of red, 256 shades of green, and 256 shades of blue. True color produces 2^{24} colors, or 16,777,216 colors. Since the human eye is only capable of discriminating a little more than 10 million colors, 24-bit color can result in more colors than the human eye can see. Other color depths above 24 bit fall into the deep color range. **Deep color** is supported by Windows 7 and later up to a 48-bit depth. This provides more intense colors and shadow. Deep color can produce a gamut of over 1 billion colors.

Bit depth also allows for transparency. With a large gamut of color, an alpha channel can be allocated. The **alpha channel** varies the opacity of the color. The alpha channel can support from full transparency all the way to full opacity. A 16-bit alpha channel can support 65,536 values of transparency.

Alpha channels can also allow for a masking color. A **masking color** is a single shade of a color that can be set to be transparent. If you have ever seen a weather report on TV, you have likely seen a masking color in use. Using a green or blue screen, called a chroma screen, will allow a background of the weather map to digitally replace the blank screen. In image creation, mask colors are typically chosen so they will not interfere with natural colors. Using a masking color such as white would be a very bad choice. If white were made to be transparent, then the white in a person's eyes and other white items would be transparent.

Vector Images

Vector images are images composed of lines, curves, and fills. Vector images do not store the color value and location of each pixel. Rather, the image is displayed based on the mathematical definition of each element in the image. In other words, in a raster image a line is composed of dots, while in a vector image the line is defined by a mathematical equation. For a vector image to be displayed, the software must rasterize the image before it is sent to the display device.

Some software programs can also convert raster images into vector images. This process is called **bitmap tracing.** The software will trace around zones that are the same or similar color to create a closed region and fill the region with a color.

A vector image can be a very small file size because the image is drawn by the computer using a mathematical formula. Since the formula draws the image, the image can be resized infinitely smaller or larger without loss of clarity, as shown in **Figure 2-2.** This is one of the biggest advantages of a vector image.

Goodheart-Willcox Publisher; image: Andreas Meyer/Shutterstock.com

Figure 2-2.

Raster images become pixelated when enlarged, but vector images can be infinitely scaled.

However, raster images offer an advantage over vector images because a vector image requires the CPU to work hard to draw the image. In the world of handheld devices with small CPUs and low memory, a vector image may have the benefit of a small file size, but may take up a large amount of CPU ability. Bitmaps do not take up a large amount of CPU ability, but have higher file size. The designer will need to understand the limits and capabilities of each device on which the image will be rendered to correctly match the file size and CPU usage to prevent lag and crashing the device.

Image File Compression

When working with images that are used on web pages or mobile devices, a designer should optimize the images. *Optimizing* an image is applying the most appropriate resolution and image file compression to achieve the smallest file size for the image quality needed. *Compression* uses mathematical formulas to approximate the location and color of each pixel and thereby reduce the total file size. Raster images are often compressed from their original raw format to reduce file size, save computer memory, and decrease download time.

A computer algorithm is used to record the pixel data in a smaller file size and then uncompress the image when it is opened in image-editing software. Almost all compression formats seek to eliminate the color values stored in the image that are beyond the capability of the human eye. The two most popular image-compression algorithms are lossy and lossless. The *lossy compression algorithm* compresses the image, but does not keep perfect image clarity. The image generally will have an acceptable appearance, but it will not be as clear when uncompressed as the original image. The *lossless compression algorithm,* or losslessly compression algorithm, compresses the image and keeps perfect clarity when uncompressed. There is a tradeoff between clarity and file size. To reduce the file size to run on a handheld device, the clarity may need to be reduced to fit the memory needs of the device and program.

File formats are needed for each type of compression so the computer will understand how to read the compressed image. **Figure 2-3** lists several popular image file formats and the compression model needed to expand the image.

Image Sizing and Resolution

When a bitmap image is enlarged, the existing pixels spread out. This *dithers* the image, which creates holes in the image where the pixels are no longer touching each other. Dithering can also occur when color is undefined in the program such as a web browser. Software uses a process called interpolation to dither an image. *Interpolation* is the refining of the space between pixels. During interpolation, the software averages the color of all pixels touching the empty space. The average color of the surrounding pixels is then assigned to the new pixel.

Part of optimizing a raster image is setting the proper resolution for the intended output. For example, an app for the iPad should have an icon that is 144 pixels × 144 pixels so the icon will properly display on the device and in the app store. A standard computer monitor has a resolution of 72 dots per inch (dpi) or 96 dpi. Making images for a website with a resolution higher than 96 dpi would not be properly optimizing the images. On the other hand, most images for print publication should be sized to specific dimensions with a resolution of 300 dpi.

File Format	Name	Image Type	Compression	Benefit
GIF	Graphic Interface Format	Raster	Lossless	Popular for use on websites; 256 colors and can be animated
PNG-8	Portable Network Graphic, 8-bit depth	Raster	Lossless	Same as GIF, but cannot be animated
PNG-24	Portable Network Graphic, 24-bit depth	Raster	Lossless	Same as PNG-8, but millions of colors and transparency options
JPEG	Joint Photographic Expert Group	Raster	Lossy	Generally offers the smallest file size
BMP	Bitmap	Raster	Run length encoded (RLE)	Device independent
TIFF	Tag Image File Format	Raster	Lossy and Lossless	Supported by most paint, imaging, and desktop publishing programs; not supported by many web browsers
RAW or CIFF	Camera Image File Format	Raster	None	Raw data at full uncompressed value obtained from a digital camera or scanner
SVG	Scalable Vector Graphic	Vector	Vector	Supported use on most browsers and mobile devices; high resolution for print, web, and mobile
AI	Adobe Illustrator	Vector	Vector	For use with Adobe Illustrator
EPS	Encapsulated PostScript	Vector	Vector	Generic vector format that can be used in any PostScript-enabled software

Goodheart-Willcox Publisher

Figure 2-3.

Common file formats for graphics.

The resolution of an image is measured in *dots per inch (dpi)* or *pixels per inch (ppi).* This measure is the number of dots or pixels along the horizontal axis of an image multiplied by the number of dots or pixels along the vertical axis of the image. An image that is one inch square with 200 pixels on each axis has horizontal and vertical resolutions of 200 dpi. If this image is stretched to two inches square without resampling, the resolution becomes 100 dpi, which results in a loss of image clarity. If an image with a horizontal resolution of 200 dpi is 5 inches wide, the horizontal dimension contains 1000 pixels (5 inches × 200 dpi = 1000 pixels).

When an image is resized, it must be *resampled* to create a new image without reducing the image resolution. Resampling interpolates the image, adding or removing pixels as needed. Most imaging software gives the designer options for selecting a resampling method. A common resampling method is bicubic. There are two variations of bicubic resampling: bicubic for reduction (downsampling) and bicubic for enlargement (upsampling). *Bicubic for reduction* is optimized for removing pixels, while *bicubic for enlargement* is optimized for creating pixels.

Fonts

A *font*, or *typeface*, is a collection of letters, numbers, and symbols that are all of the same design or style. The font can be important in conveying meaning in a design project. Text set in one font may communicate elegance, while the same text set in a different font may communicate excitement or tension.

The two basic designs of font or typeface are serif and sans serif. *Serifs* are decorative marks at the ends of letters, as shown in **Figure 2-4.** The word *sans* means without, so *sans serif* means without serif. There is much debate over which is more readable. Traditionally, serif type is used for long passages where readability is important, such as books, while sans serif type is used when legibility is important, such as street signs. However, there is no clear agreement among experts as to the significance between serif and sans serif type when it comes to readability and legibility. It is generally thought that a sans serif typeface promotes the feeling of security, trust, and strength, which is why this type is typically used in logos and headlines.

Other typefaces that fall outside of serif or sans serif classification include novelty, ornate, handwritten, script, and ornamental. These are used as decoration or as an attention item on a page and should not be used when creating the body text. In addition to being hard to read, they may have the added problem of not being installed on the user's computer, which is important in web page design. If a device does not have a specified font, whether decorative, serif, or sans serif, it will be displayed in a substitute font.

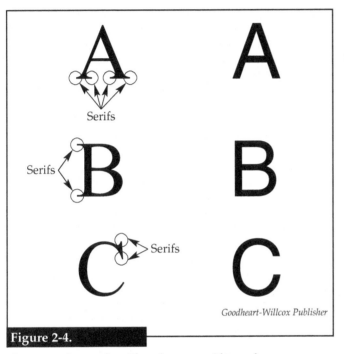

Goodheart-Willcox Publisher

Figure 2-4.
A comparison of serif and sans serif typefaces.

Lesson Review

Vocabulary

In a word processing document or on a sheet of paper, list all of the *key terms* in this lesson. Place each term on a separate line. Then, write a definition for each term using your own words. You will continue to build this terminology dictionary throughout this certification guide.

Review Questions

Answer the following questions. These questions are aligned to questions in the certification exam. Answering these questions will help prepare you to take the exam.

1. Which raster image file type supports millions of colors and transparency?

2. List six common raster image file types.

_____

_____

3. List three common vector image file types.

_____

_____

4. Which color model and resolution (in dpi) would be best for an image used on a website that is viewed from a desktop computer?

_____

_____

5. Describe how an alpha channel and masking color control image transparency.

_____

_____

_____

_____

6. Which type of image is composed of lines, curves, and fills?

_____

7. Describe bitmap tracing.

_____

_____

8. Compare and contrast raster images with vector images.

_____

_____

_____

_____

9. What are the two aspects of optimizing a raster image for use on a website or handheld device?

_____

_____

10. Which two file formats shown in Figure 2-3 offer the best flexibility if an image needs to be used for print, web, and mobile advertisement?

_____

11. A digital designer is going to edit an image that will be used in both print and web formats. In which color model should the designer save the image?

_____

12. A client wants you to create a leader-board banner ad for a website. The standard size of a leader-board banner is 728 pixels wide and 90 pixels tall. If a computer display is 72 dpi, how large is the leader-board banner in inches?

13. Which bicubic resampling method is best if enlarging an image from 300 pixels wide to 800 pixels wide?

_____

14. Describe the difference between a serif and sans serif font.

_____

_____

15. Which font design is generally thought to instill trust in the reader?

_____

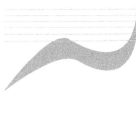

Lesson 3
Exploring the Photoshop Interface

Objectives

Students will identify the responsibilities of a digital artist. Student will describe preproduction interviews. Students will explain preproduction deliverables. Students will discuss conversion of traditional artwork to digital artwork. Students will differentiate soft proofs and hard proofs. Students will summarize how to collaborate on a Photoshop project. Students will describe the Photoshop workspace. Students will identify Photoshop tools and options. Students will use Photoshop panels. Students will explain layers. Students will import an image into a Photoshop document. Students will crop and straighten an image. Students will discuss content-aware smart tools. Students will discuss the **Properties** panel.

Situation

The Nocturnal Interactive Computer Entertainment (NICE) company is hiring a new apprentice for its digital image department. You have interviewed for the job and have been given a chance to participate in the apprentice program. To be hired as a full-time artist with the company, you will have to pass the Adobe Certified Associate (ACA) Photoshop Creative Cloud industry certification exam. The first step in preparing for the exam is to gain experience using the functions of the software and becoming informed of the needs of a digital art project.

Reading Materials

A rewarding career is possible in digital image production. Many industries need quality employees who can take client information and produce the desired image. Professionals use Adobe Photoshop for game design, web design, print design, digital production, photography, and many other uses. Those who are competent using Photoshop should be able to have rich careers creating visually stunning work. *Industry certification* provides proof to employers that an individual has achieved a certain level of qualification and aptitude in a specific area, such as software use.

Digital Artist

At a design studio, a Photoshop-certified employee is expected to know more than just the software functions. The most valuable employees can take control of a project and create a finished work to the client's expectations. As a digital designer or digital artist, you will be fully responsible for creating sample graphics and the final image of the project. Working with the client will allow you to narrow your focus on producing the best graphics for the job.

Preproduction Interview

When working with a client, it is important to have a full understanding of what he or she expects. You should conduct *preproduction interviews* with the client to brainstorm ideas and fully communicate the goals for the finished product. A preproduction interview takes place before any production work begins. If you start working without this important step, the client may be dissatisfied with the result and you would have to redo the project. In the professional world, you are paid by the client, and the client will not pay for unsatisfactory work that does not meet the specified goals. Working with the client in a preproduction interview, you will need to identify the client goals and target market.

The *client goals* set the direction of the creative work. The client is paying you to create something to meet a goal, often attracting customers. This means the graphics and layout need to meet these goals or the client will feel he or she did not receive the service for which payment was made. Client goals can include what the graphics will be used for, such as packaging, website, billboard, employee handbook, etc., and the specifications of the graphics. The specifications for an image used on a billboard will be much different than for an image used on a website. Additionally, the client may have goals of informing or attracting attention. The use of color is important in attracting attention, while color in informational items may have little value.

The *target market* is the group of people for whom the work is intended. The target market for a cartoon-style image is likely very different from the target market of a photorealistic image. If the target market is children, an advertising project may have little or no text, may contain fantasy characters, and may use bright colors. If the audience is college graduates, the advertisement may contain large blocks of text and photorealistic images or photographs.

Preproduction Deliverables

Before starting to build a project in Photoshop, preproduction deliverables should be defined and created. *Preproduction deliverables* include sketches, mockups, and specifications. From the client interviews, you can work out the use of the images and find out the quality needed. *Sketching* the design is creating a freehand drawing of the design, which is always a great way to show the client that you understand what he or she wants and how to create the finished product. *Mockups* are physical models of the design. For example, if the client wants a cereal box, it may be helpful to create a preliminary mockup of how the design will be placed on the physical box. *Specifications* include the scope of the work to be done and the deadline. The *deadline* is the date the project must be delivered to the client.

Scope defines how the image will be output in final form and the intended use. Is the image going to go on a web page or is it going to be on a roadside billboard? The difference between these final forms greatly affects the way the digital design work is done. Another part of the scope is what the client intends to do with the image. For example, if the client wants to use an image for a global campaign, then the image needs to take into consideration *cultural differences* between America and the areas where the image will be used. Some objects, gestures, or actions are acceptable in America, but offensive in other cultures. In an Arab country, for example, showing the bottom of a foot is offensive. So an image of people at the beach intended to be shown in that market should not contain visible feet bottoms. Once again, taking the time to interview the client and explore all wants and needs will help avoid mistakes.

Conversion of Traditional Artwork and Printed Photographs

The digital artist may need to perform a *conversion* to change physical art into digital format, or to *digitize* the artwork. Typically, conversions are performed on traditional artwork such as drawings, paintings, and continuous tone (nondigital) photographs. When performing these conversions, the most important consideration is the technology needed to properly convert the image to the best quality of digital image for the application. A sketch may simply need to be photographed by a digital camera to make it a digital sketch. A digital camera takes a photograph, but in digital form instead of on film. A high-quality painting might need a digital scanner to capture the quality of the image. A *digital scanner* passes light over an image, similar to a photocopy machine, and digitally records each point of color. Other items that may need to be converted into digital form are photographic slides or other nonstandard images. *Slides* are photographs printed on transparent film from which the image is projected onto a screen to view it. Special equipment is often needed to properly convert slides to digital format.

Whenever possible, have the client submit the images in digital format so you do not have to do the conversions. This will save you time and also places the responsibility for the quality of the conversion on the client. The client can also save money by not having to pay you to do the conversions. However, in many cases the client will not have the ability to do the conversion or the technical knowledge to provide the proper quality.

Proofs

Before creating the final output in all required formats, the client should view and approve the work. The output you provide the client is a proof. A *proof* is a copy of final output created for approval. When the client signs off on a proof, he or she is giving approval to create the final output needed. A *hard proof* is a physical proof printed on paper or various other substrates, while a *soft proof* is viewed on the computer. You may want to use Photoshop to do a soft proof preview. An advantage of a soft proof or electronic proof over a hard proof is the ability to quickly see how the image would look in different outputs. Changing color models or output devices will change the overall look of the image in the soft proof. To do the same thing with a hard proof, a new proof would have to be pulled for each version. Soft proofs are also a cost-saving device, as hard proofs can be expensive to generate.

Collaboration and Sharing Assets

Many times, you will be collaborating with other designers during a project. Using the Adobe Creative Cloud and Adobe Bridge will help organize and share work. *Adobe Creative Cloud* offers a way to share files, give feedback, and save settings across devices. *Adobe Bridge* provides a convenient portal for storing design elements, such as images, used in more than one Adobe program. Images created in Photoshop can be embedded or linked into another program. An *embedded* image becomes part of that document. Think of it as a copy of the image file. A *linked* image is a placeholder space added to a document, but the original image is stored outside of the program. A linked image can be edited and saved in Photoshop and those changes will be reflected in any document to which the image is linked. For example, an image altered in Photoshop will be used in Adobe Dreamweaver to create a website. Adobe Bridge allows the image to be placed in the Dreamweaver web page. The Photoshop artist can later manipulate the image and save it in Adobe Bridge. The image is automatically updated in the Dreamweaver web page. Adobe Bridge provides a convenient way to manage, open, and view design assets and files.

How to Begin

1. Before beginning this lesson, download the needed files from the student companion website located at www.g-wlearning.com, and unzip them into your working folder.

2. Launch Photoshop Creative Cloud.

3. Click **New...** in the **File** pull-down menu to begin a new document. The **New Document** dialog box is displayed, as shown in **Figure 3-1.**

4. Click the **Print** link at the top of the dialog box. A list of preset templates suitable for print-based projects is displayed.

5. Click the Letter preset tile. This template will create a document that is 8.5″ × 11″ (letter-size paper) at a resolution of 300 dots per inch (dpi). Notice these settings are automatically filled in on the right-hand side of the dialog box.

6. Click the document name on the right-hand side of the dialog box, which is currently Untitled-1, to make it editable. Change the name to Workspace.

7. Click the **Color Mode** drop-down arrow, and click **RGB Color** in the drop-down list to select the RGB color model.

TIP
After selecting a preset tile, the default settings can be overridden using the text boxes on the right-hand side of the **New Document** dialog box.

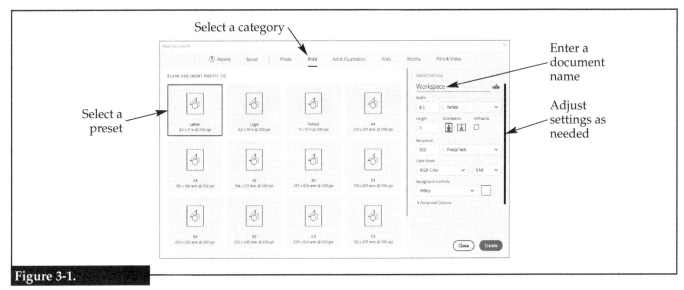

Figure 3-1.

Starting a new document in Photoshop.

8. Click the drop-down arrow to the right of the **Color Mode** drop-down arrow, and click **8 bit** in the drop-down list to set the bit depth for the color model.

9. Click the **Create** button to accept all other values and open the new document.

10. Click **Save As...** in the **File** pull-down menu. The **Save As** dialog box is displayed, which is a standard save-type dialog box.

11. Navigate to your working folder.

12. Click the **New Folder** link at the top of the dialog box. A new folder is created in the current folder and ready to be named.

13. Name the new folder Photoshop Working Folder.

14. Navigate to the new folder.

15. Click in the **File name:** text box, and enter Workspace.

16. Click the **Save as type:** drop-down arrow, and click **Photoshop (*.PSD; *.PDD; *.PSDT)** in the drop-down list. This is Photoshop's native file format.

17. Click the **Save** button to save the document as a PSD file in your Photoshop working folder.

Workspace

A *workspace* is the layout of the toolbars, panels, and document on the screen. Changing the layout by moving panels, adding more tools, rearranging panels, or otherwise changing the screen setup changes the workspace. A workspace can be customized to display the toolbars and panels in different locations to help the designer perform best. You may also create custom views by dragging the workspace tools to different locations and saving the workspace.

Review the location and name of each tool shown in **Figure 3-2.** These will be referred to by name throughout the lesson set. Note: the color scheme shown in the screen captures in this guide has been changed to a lighter scheme for easier viewing.

The **Menu** bar holds commands in a pull-down menu format. Click a pull-down menu to see the commands it contains, and then click a command to activate it. The **Menu** bar is available in the PC version of Photoshop.

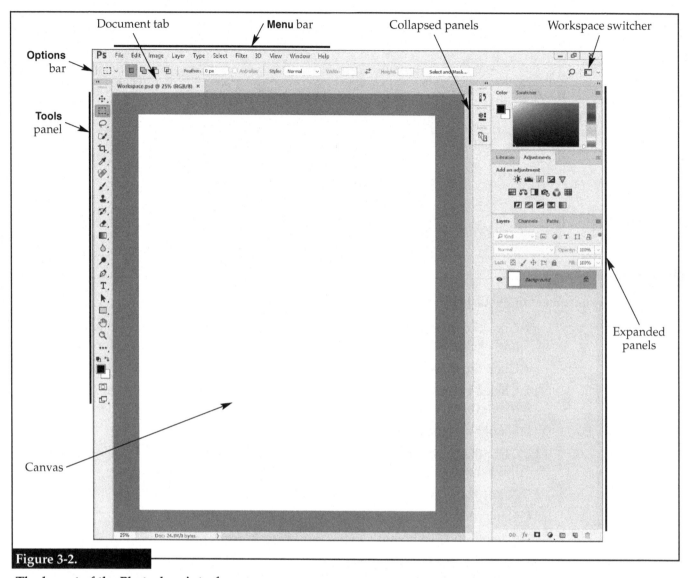

Figure 3-2.

The layout of the Photoshop interface.

The **Options** bar contains a contextual toolbar. A contextual toolbar, panel, or menu contains options or features for the active tool. For example, if the brush tool is selected, the **Options** bar displays settings for brush size and other options.

The **Tools** panel holds the common tools used to design in Photoshop. Tools are organized on the panel by function with a line separating each group.

Photoshop makes use of panels. A *panel* is a small window that holds commands or options. A panel may be in a group by command function. A designer can arrange the panels in any configuration. The panels can even be moved from one panel group to another. Panels may be expanded with the commands visible or collapsed. Collapsed panels have been minimized to icons to save space on the screen. Clicking a panel icon will expand the panel.

The *canvas* is the area where the image or design is created. Just like the canvas used by a painter, only the work on the canvas can be printed. Text and image assets can be combined and layered on the canvas to create a composite image. Outside the canvas is the pasteboard. Nothing can be created on the pasteboard in Photoshop.

The *document tab* contains the document. The designer can have multiple documents open in Photoshop at the same time. Each document will have a separate document tab. The designer can navigate between open documents by simply clicking the different document tabs. Dragging a document tab off the document tab area opens the document in a separate window.

18. Locate the workspace switcher in the top-right corner of the screen. Click the workspace switcher, and click **Essentials** in the drop-down menu. Notice the other standardized workspaces that are available in the drop-down menu.

19. Click the bar at the top of the **Tools** panel, hold, and drag the panel to the middle of the screen. The panel is now *floating*.

20. Click the collapsed **History** panel on the right-hand side of the screen. The panel is expanded.

21. Click the workspace switcher, and click **Reset Essentials** in the drop-down menu. The workspace is reset to the default state of the Essentials workspace. Notice how the panels are restored to their original locations. Unless instructed to change workspaces, use the default Essentials workspace throughout this guide.

Tools and Options

The Photoshop **Tools** panel contains a set of tools organized into groups. Some tools have similar tools hidden under the shown tool. A black triangle at the bottom-right corner of a tool indicates a flyout. Clicking and holding the button displays the flyout toolbar that contains additional tools.

22. Identify each of the tools shown in **Figure 3-3**. Hover the cursor over each tool in the **Tools** panel to display the name, and record the name of each tool in the figure.

45	Icon	Name		Icon	Name
1.			9.		
2.			10.		
3.			11.		
4.			12.		
5.			13.		
6.			14.		
7.			15.		
8.			16.		

(Continued)

Figure 3-3.

Write the name of each tool identified here.

	Icon	Name		Icon	Name
17.			36.		
18.			37.		
19.			38.		
20.			39.		
21.			40.		
22.			41.		
23.			42.		
24.			43.		
25.			44.		
26.			45.		
27.			46.		
28.			47.		
29.			48.		
30.			49.		
31.			50.		
32.			51.		
33.			52.		
34.			53.		
35.			54.		

(Continued)

Figure 3-3.

(Continued.)

	Icon	Name		Icon	Name
55.			60.		
56.			61.		
57.			62.		
58.			63.		
59.			64.		

Figure 3-3.

(Continued.)

Rectangle Tool

23. Click the **Rectangle Tool** button in the **Tools** panel. The tool is activated, and the cursor changes to a crosshair or plus sign.

24. Click anywhere on the canvas, hold, and drag to draw a rectangle of any size. When the mouse button is released, the rectangle is created and automatically filled with the foreground color, as shown in **Figure 3-4.**

25. Click the **Fill:** color swatch on the **Options** bar, and click the red color swatch in the drop-down menu. The rectangle is filled with that color.

26. Click the **Stroke:** color swatch on the **Options** bar, and click the black color swatch in the drop-down menu. The stroke, or outline, of the rectangle is set to black where previously it had no color. Click on any blank space on the **Options** bar to close the drop-down menu.

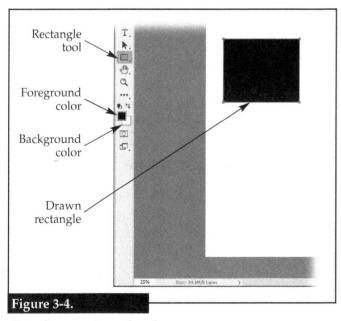

Rectangle tool

Foreground color

Background color

Drawn rectangle

Figure 3-4.

Drawing a rectangular shape.

27. Hover the cursor over the text box to the right of the **Stroke:** color swatch on the **Options** bar. The help text states Set shape stroke width. The *weight* is the thickness of a line. If the drop-down arrow is clicked, a slider is displayed that can be dragged to change the value, or a value can be directly entered in the text box.

28. Enter 10 pt in the stroke width text box. This sets the stroke to exactly 10 points wide. Point and pica are common units of measurement used in the graphic design industry. One *point* is 1/72 of an inch, or approximately 0.0139″. One *pica* is equal to 12 points, and there are six picas per inch.

29. Click the drop-down arrow to the right of the stroke width drop-down arrow. The help text for this drop-down arrow is Set shape stroke type. A drop-down menu is displayed containing options for the stroke type or style.

30. Choose the dotted line option in the drop-down menu. The stroke is changed from a solid line to a dotted line.

31. In the same drop-down menu, click the **Align:** drop-down arrow, and click the middle option in the drop-down list. The line is shifted so it is centered on the edge of the rectangle. The center of each dot is on the edge of the rectangle.

32. Click in the **W:** text box (width) on the **Options** bar, and enter 1000 px. The width of the rectangle is changed to 1000 pixels. *Px* stands for pixels.

33. Click in the **H:** text box, and enter 800 px to set the height of the rectangle.

Using Panels

34. In the expanded panels on the right side of the screen, click the **Color** tab to display that panel. This panel is displayed by default. Notice that the **Color** panel contains a mixer to define a color. Additionally, there is a color spectrum bar on the right of the panel that can be used to pick a color.

35. Click anywhere on the color spectrum bar. Notice the foreground color swatch displays the color, both in the **Color** panel and on the **Tools** panel.

36. Click the **Swatches** tab in the expanded panels to display that panel. Swatches are small samples of color. A paint store has swatches of paint colors on paper for customers to see the how the color will look.

37. Move the cursor over the color swatches. Notice the cursor changes to an eyedropper to indicate a color can be selected. This cursor is called the *color picker.* The name of each color is shown as help text next to the cursor.

38. Click the **Adjustments** tab in the expanded panels to display that panel. Notice there are several tools on the **Adjustments** panel that make adjustments to the image. Hover the cursor over each button to see the name of each tool.

39. Click the **Image** pull-down menu at the top of the screen, and then click **Adjustments** to display a cascading menu. Notice this menu contains many of the same adjustment tools shown in the **Adjustments** panel.

40. Leave the **Adjustments** cascading menu displayed, and move the cursor over each tool in the top row of the **Adjustments** panel. Identify which button corresponds to each menu entry. Note: there are more commands in the **Adjustments** cascading menu than there are buttons in the **Adjustments** panel.

The adjustment tools are available in two locations for a very important reason. Changes made using the commands in the pull-down menu are destructive changes, while changes made with the panels are nondestructive changes. *Destructive changes* directly alter the original image. *Nondestructive changes* are changes added to a new layer and do not alter the original image. So any changes made using the **Adjustments** panel will add a new adjustment layer to the image. Layers are discussed in detail later.

41. Click **Window>Styles** on the **Menu** bar. The **Styles** panel is displayed in the same location as the **Adjustments** panel. Styles are preset or custom adjustments that can be applied to objects and layers.

42. Click and hold the **Styles** tab, and drag it up to the expanded panels above it, and drop it to the right of the **Swatches** tab, as shown in **Figure 3-5.** Panels can be moved around the workspace to suit your preference.

43. Click any style in the **Styles** panel to see how the rectangle changes. Note: the Rectangle 1 layer must be selected (highlighted) in the **Layers** panel.

44. Click the panel menu button in the top-right corner of the **Styles** panel. Each expanded panel has this button. The panel menu includes settings that will change the information displayed in the panel.

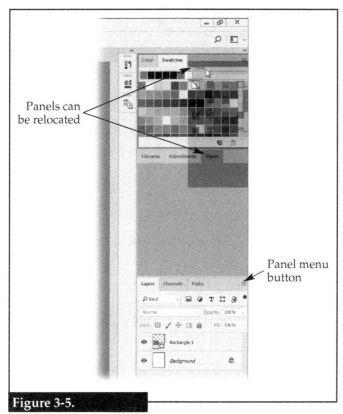

Figure 3-5.

Panels are a main interface for tools and commands in Photoshop.

45. Click **Textures** in the panel menu.

46. When asked if you want to replace the current styles, click the **OK** button. The swatches in the **Styles** panel are now for textures. Textures are styles that simulate raised and lowered effects on the image.

47. Click any swatch to apply that texture style to the selected rectangle.

48. Applying what you have learned, use the panel menu to select other categories of styles, and apply different styles to the rectangle.

49. Click **Reset Styles...** in the panel menu to return to the default styles.

50. Click the **Default Style (None)** swatch to clear all styles from the rectangle, then click the **Sunspots (texture)** swatch to apply that style.

Introduction to Layers

The **Layers** panel is one of the most important features in Photoshop. A *layer* is like a sheet of paper, and multiple sheets, or layers, can be stacked on top of each other. Photoshop builds an image using multiple layers. When the image is finished, the layers can be flattened to create a single image, but in many cases the layers are retained in the final output. There are many different options for working with layers that are covered throughout the lessons in this guide.

51. Click the **Layers** tab in the expanded panels to display that panel. This panel is displayed by default.

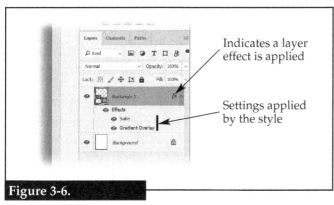

Figure 3-6.

Effects applied to a layer appear below the layer name in the Layers panel.

52. Click the Rectangle 1 layer in the **Layers** panel to select it. Notice Effects, Satin, and Gradient Overlay branches appear below the title of the layer, as shown in **Figure 3-6.** These are the settings applied by the style to change the appearance of the layer.

53. Using the **Styles** panel, change the style to Blue Glass (button). Notice the settings that now appear as branches below the layer name.

54. Click the eye icon next to the Bevel & Emboss effect. Clicking the eye icon turns off the effect. Notice how the rectangle is no longer beveled.

55. Click to the left of the Bevel & Emboss effect, where eye icon was displayed. The eye icon appears and the effect is turned on. The rectangle is beveled.

56. Click the collapsed **History** panel to expand it. The collapsed panels are located to the top-left of the expanded panels, as shown in **Figure 3-2.** Notice the panel expands outward to the left.

57. Click the **Expand Panels** button (<<) above the collapsed panels area. All collapsed panels are expanded. However, notice how the working area, the canvas, is much smaller now.

58. Click the **Collapse to Icons** button (>>) above the **History** panel. The **History** and **Properties** panels are collapsed. The other expanded panels can be similarly collapsed, if you ever need to do so.

59. Applying what you have learned, reset Essentials workspace to the default state.

60. Applying what you have learned, click the eye icon to hide the Rectangle 1 layer. The canvas should appear empty, but the Rectangle 1 layer is not deleted.

Importing an Image

61. Click **File>Place Embedded...** on the **Menu** bar. A standard open dialog box is displayed.

62. Navigate to your working folder, select the Wood image file, and click the **Place** button.

63. When the wood image appears on the canvas, resizing handles are displayed around its perimeter. Press the [Enter] key to complete the paste and apply the image to the canvas.

64. Notice a Wood layer has been added to the **Layers** panel. The name of this layer is based on the file name of the applied image.

Crop and Straighten

Images often require straightening and removing of unneeded areas. To *crop* an image is to remove the part of the image that falls outside of a selected area. A designer may crop an image to change the focal point of the image or to remove part of the image that should not be seen. Straightening involves rotating the image so vertical lines appear vertical and horizontal lines appear horizontal.

Crop Tool

65. Click the **Crop Tool** button in the **Tools** panel.

Straighten

66. Click the **Straighten** button on the **Options** bar.

67. Using the diagonal gaps between the wood planks as a guide, click and hold at the bottom-left of one of the gaps, and drag to draw a diagonal line to the top-right of the gap. When the mouse button is released, Photoshop will straighten the image. Notice that part of the image is dimmed or grayed out. This is the area that will be removed if you complete the operation. Also notice that rotating the image causes part of the background, which is white, to be visible. Photoshop does not create new parts of the image to fill in these areas.

TIP
The entire image is rotated when straightening an image, not just the current layer.

68. Click the commit button (check mark) on the **Options** bar to complete the operation. The rotation is made permanent, and the areas outside of the canvas are cropped (removed).

69. Click **View>Fit on Screen** on the **Menu** bar to maximize the zoom. This displays the image as large as possible while still allowing you to see the entire image.

Using Content-Aware Smart Tools

Smart tools have an element of artificial intelligence. A content-aware smart tool attempts to make intelligent decisions regarding changes to the content of the image. For example, suppose a photograph is of three birds on a background. If the image is scaled up normally, the birds would be increased in size and spaced out farther. However, the **Content-Aware Scale Tool** attempts to keep the birds the same size as the image is scaled. The **Content-Aware Move Tool** could be used to move the birds to a new location on the background. The tool would attempt to automatically blend the surrounding area to make the image seem unaltered. The **Content-Aware Move Tool** has two modes: move and extend. The move mode cuts the selection and moves it to another area of the image. The hole created by cutting the selection will automatically blend and the moved selection will also automatically blend. The extend mode copies the selection instead of moving it. Content-aware smart tools can save a designer a lot of time.

Elliptical Marquee Tool

TIP

The selection can be moved by moving the cursor over the selection, clicking, and dragging the marquee.

Content-Aware Move Tool

70. Make sure the Wood layer is selected, then click the **Elliptical Marquee Tool** button in the **Tools** panel.

71. Locate the line of bolts along the left-hand side of the image and the hole near the bottom. Click above and to the left of the bolt just above the hole, hold down the [Shift] key, and drag to create a circular selection. A selection is indicated by a marquee, which is often referred to as marching ants because white and black dashes rotate around the selection like ants marching. If the [Shift] key is not held down, an elliptical selection can be made. The selection should include the bolt and part of the surrounding wood. If you need to redo the selection, press the [Ctrl][Z] key combination to undo the action, and then try again.

72. Click the **Content-Aware Move Tool** button in the **Tools** panel.

73. In the **Options** bar, click the **Mode:** button, and click **Move** in the drop-down menu.

74. Click inside the selection. A message appears indicating the object must be rasterized. Click the **OK** button to continue.

75. Drag the selection down to cover the hole, and then click the commit button (check mark) on the **Options** bar to complete the operation. Photoshop begins calculating how to blend the bolt into the surrounding image. This may take some time, depending on the speed of your computer. Notice how the move mode removes the bolt from its original location and placed it in the new location, as shown in **Figure 3-7**. The original location is filled with a wood pattern. Also notice how the selection remains active.

76. Applying what you have learned, change the **Content-Aware Move Tool** mode to extend.

77. Drag the selection to the hole on the right-hand side of the image, and commit the operation. Notice how extend mode copies the bolt, but does not remove it from its original location. The copy is blended into the wood in the new location.

78. Click **Deselect** in the **Select** pull-down menu or press the [Ctrl][D] key combination to cancel the selection.

Working with Selections

So far, you have used basic selections. There are other selection tools, which include the **Lasso Tool**, **Polygonal Lasso Tool**, and **Magnetic Selection Tool**. Additionally, areas can be added to or removed from a selection.

Rectangular Marquee Tool

79. With the Wood layer selected, click the **Rectangular Marquee Tool** button in the **Tools** panel.

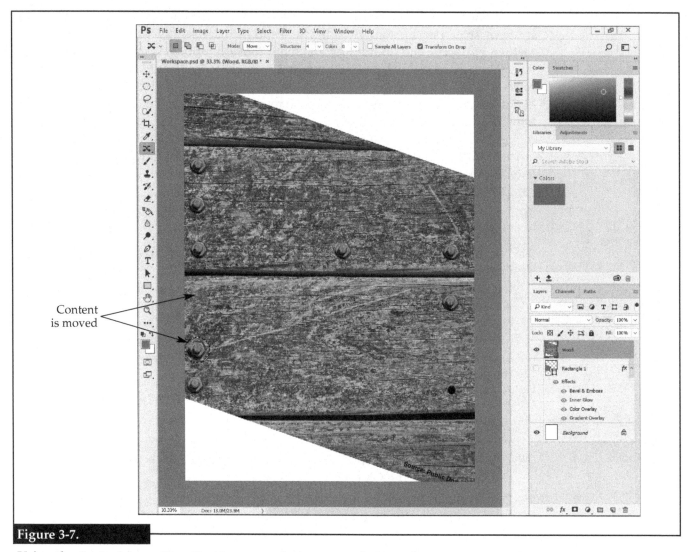

Content is moved

Figure 3-7.

Using the **Content-Aware Move Tool** to move a feature on a photograph.

80. Click and drag a rectangular marquee around the two middle wood planks. Since the image was straightened, some of the background (white) will be included in the selection.

Subtract from Selection

81. Applying what you have learned, activate the **Elliptical Marquee Tool**. In the **Options** bar, click the **Subtract from Selection** button.

82. Draw an oval marquee within the rectangular selection over where the rectangle is located on the layer beneath (that layer is hidden, so you will not be able to see the rectangle). There should be two marquees, the rectangular marquee and the elliptical marquee. The area within the elliptical marquee is removed from the selection.

83. Applying what you have learned, turn on the visibility of the Rectangle 1 layer.

Add Layer Mask

84. Click the **Add Layer Mask** button at the bottom of the **Layers** panel. This changes the selected area into a layer mask. A *mask* controls areas of transparency for the layer. Part of the rectangle on the layer beneath should be visible, as shown in **Figure 3-8.** Also notice areas of the Wood layer outside of the rectangular marquee are no longer visible. In this case, the mask is a vector mask. A *vector mask* is created with vector objects, which allows the mask to

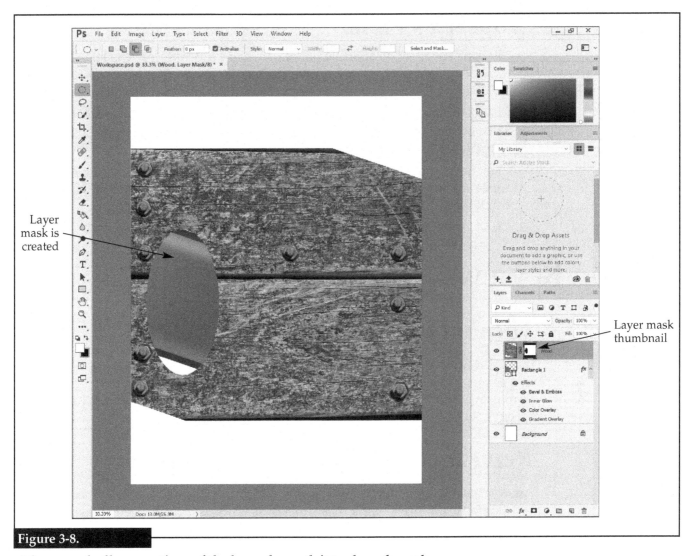

Layer
mask is
created

Layer mask
thumbnail

Figure 3-8.

A layer mask allows portions of the layers beneath it to show through.

be resolution-independent and have clean edges. A *layer mask* is created with pixel-based bitmap objects and is resolution-dependent.

85. Right-click on the layer mask thumbnail in the **Layers** panel, and click **Add Mask to Selection** in the shortcut menu. The mask is converted into a selection. If there had been an existing selection, the area of the mask would have been added to the selection.

86. Click the **Lasso Tool** button on the **Tools** panel.

87. In the **Options** bar, click the **Add to Selection** button.

88. Click and drag to draw an irregular selection completely around the hole in the mask. When the mouse button is released, the selection is closed. Since the mode is adding to the selection, the remaining selection should be the original rectangular selection. However, notice the mask has not changed.

89. Applying what you have learned, deselect everything.

Lasso Tool

Add to Selection

Properties Panel

90. Click the collapsed **Properties** panel to expand it. Make sure the layer mask thumbnail for the Wood layer is selected so the property settings for this mask are displayed. A dashed line around the thumbnail means it is selected.

91. Change the value in the **Feather:** text box to 50 pixels either by entering the value or dragging the slider. This will apply a feathered edge to the mask so the transition is not a sharp edge.

92. Click **Save** in the **File** pull-down menu to save the document. If a message appears asking to maximize compatibility, check the **Maximize Compatibility** check box and click the **OK** button.

93. Close Photoshop.

Lesson Review

Vocabulary

In a word processing document or on a sheet of paper, list all of the *key terms* in this lesson. Place each term on a separate line. Then, write a definition for each term using your own words. You will continue to build this terminology dictionary throughout this certification guide.

Review Questions

Answer the following questions. These questions are aligned to questions in the certification exam. Answering these questions will help prepare you to take the exam.

1. In a design project, what two types of graphics or images is the digital artist responsible for creating?

2. What should be done to determine what the client wants before any work begins?

3. Why are client goals and target audience important considerations for an image?

4. During the client interview, the client suggested the major colors to use in a logo design. When you begin working on the logo, you notice the colors will not look good together. What should you do as the next step in the design process?

5. What is included in preproduction deliverables?

6. A web designer wants to include an image on a web page that will display a weekly advertisement. The image will be updated each Monday. Should the designer choose an embedded or linked image? Why?

_____

_____

7. What should be considered when preparing an image to be used internationally?

_____

_____

8. Describe how a digital scanner would digitize an oil painting.

_____

_____

9. Why does a digital artist get the proof images signed?

_____

_____

10. What are two advantages of soft proofs over hard proofs?

_____

_____

11. Which part of the Photoshop interface contains commands in pull-down menus?

_____

12. Once a tool is selected, where are additional tool settings and contextual information available?

_____

13. What is the difference between a collapsed panel and an expanded panel?

_____

_____

14. What is the term for the area where the image is created?

_____

15. How would a designer know there are tools contained in a flyout on the **Tools** panel?

_____

_____

16. What is the stroke of a shape?

_____

17. Which panel contains a mixer to define a color?

_____

18. Which panel contains tools that create a layer to make adjustments to the image?

_____

19. Different texture styles are located in which panel?

_____

20. Briefly describe how to straighten an image using the **Crop Tool**.

_____

_____

21. How do you set the maximum zoom level while still being able to see the entire image?

_____

_____

22. Which mode of the **Content-Aware Move Tool** is used to copy a selection?

_____

23. Which mode of the **Content-Aware Move Tool** is used to cut a selection?

_____

24. Which selection tool option is used to add missing parts to an active selection?

_____

25. What is the difference between a vector mask and a layer mask?

_____

_____

Lesson 4
Editing Images

Objectives

Students will copy and paste an image. Students will fit an image to size. Students will isolate an image element. Students will create a layer from a selection. Students will apply layer styles. Students will add to an existing image. Students will adjust an image. Students will manage layers. Students will manage the workspace.

Situation

The Nocturnal Interactive Computer Entertainment (NICE) company wants you to create a superhero image that will be used in different print and digital media. In the process, you will gain experience using Photoshop to edit images.

How to Begin

1. Before beginning this lesson, download the needed files from the student companion website located at www.g-wlearning.com, and unzip them into your working folder.

2. Launch Adobe Photoshop.

3. Click **New…** in the **File** pull-down menu to display the **New** dialog box.

4. Applying what you have learned, name the document *LastName*_Hero_1 and set the color model to 8-bit RGB.

5. Click the drop-down arrow to the right of the **Width:** text box, and click **Inches** in the drop-down list. Click in the **Width:** text box, and enter 6. This specifies the width of the document as 6".

6. Click in the **Height:** text box, and enter 10. This specifies the height of the document as 10".

7. Click in the **Resolution:** text box, and enter 72. Make sure the drop-down arrow to the right of the **Resolution:** text box is set to **Pixels/Inch**.

8. Click the **Background Contents:** drop-down arrow, and click **white** in the drop-down menu.

9. Click the **Create** button to create the new document.

10. Save the document as *LastName*_Hero_1.psd in your working folder.

Copying and Pasting an Image

Notice the canvas area is filled with white. Also notice the **Layers** panel displays Background and shows a thumbnail of the canvas. You will now paste the superhero image into this document.

11. Open the Hero file from your working folder.

12. Applying what you have learned, select the entire image.

13. Click **Copy** in the **Edit** pull-down menu.

14. Close the Hero file by clicking the close button (X) on the document name tab.

15. With the Hero_1 document active, click **Paste** in the **Edit** pull-down menu. Notice the copied image is pasted as Layer 1 as shown in **Figure 4-1**.

Fitting an Image to Size

Right now, the superhero does not fit the canvas and is not at the correct rotation. The pasted image needs to be modified to make it fit correctly on the canvas.

16. Make sure Layer 1 is selected in the **Layers** panel, and then click **Edit>Transform>Rotate 90° Counter Clockwise** in the **Menu** bar. The layer is rotated to the right by 90 degrees, but notice the canvas is not rotated.

17. Click the **Move Tool** button on the **Tools** panel. This tool moves everything on the current layer.

18. Click the image, hold, and drag so the superhero is centered in the canvas. Notice the image is larger than the canvas with some extra elements in addition to the superhero. Some changes need to be made to the image.

TIP
The [Ctrl][C] key combination can be used to copy a selection. The [Ctrl][V] key combination can be used to paste content from the system clipboard.

Move Tool

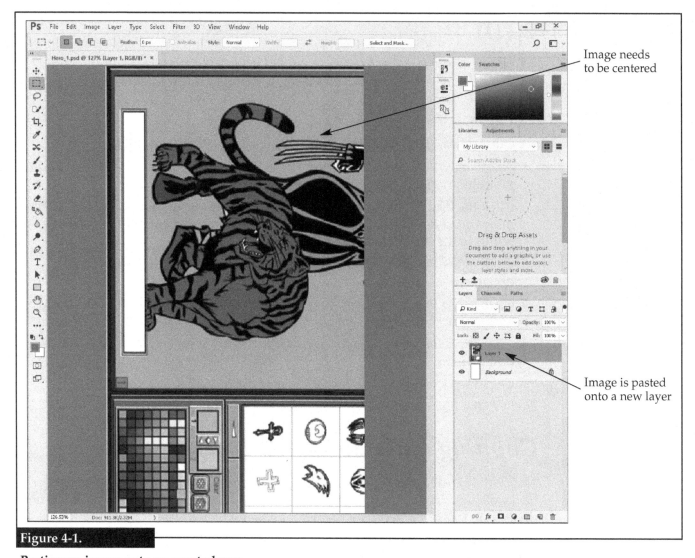

Image needs to be centered

Image is pasted onto a new layer

Figure 4-1.

Pasting an image onto an empty layer.

19. Click **Reveal All** in the **Image** pull-down menu. This shows the entire image by resizing the canvas to fit the dimensions of the pasted image.

20. Click the **Crop Tool** button on the **Tools** panel. Click on the image and drag a rectangular box around the superhero. You can partially enclose the desired area, and then resize the box by dragging the edges. Use the scroll bars as needed to see the image and define the rectangular region.

21. On the **Options** bar, check the **Delete Cropped Pixels** check box. When checked, anything outside the crop box will be deleted. If unchecked, the area outside the box will be preserved, but hidden.

Set Additional Crop Options

22. Click the **Set Additional Crop Options** button on the **Options** bar. A drop-down menu is displayed, as shown in **Figure 4-2.**

23. Click the **Color:** drop-down arrow, and click **Custom** in the drop-down list. The **Color Picker** dialog box is displayed.

24. In the **Color Picker** dialog box, click in the **#** text box at the bottom, enter FF0000, and click the **OK** button. FF0000 is the hexadecimal code for red. This color will be placed over the area to be removed by cropping, which is called the shield.

25. Click in the **Opacity:** text box, and enter 90%. This sets the transparency of the color to almost opaque, but part of the image is still visible through the color.

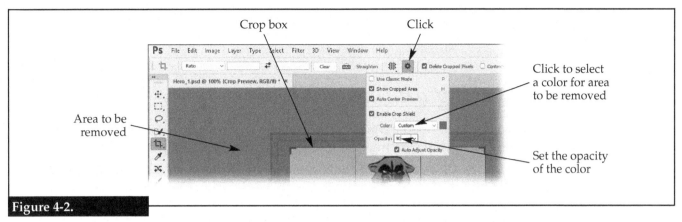

Figure 4-2.

Cropping an image.

**Overlay
Options**

26. Click the **Set Additional Crop Options** button to close the drop-down menu. Refine the crop box as needed. There should be about a quarter inch of space between the character and the crop box, except at the bottom where the box should be at the bottom of the tiger's feet.

27. Click the **Overlay Options:** button on the **Options** bar, and click **Golden Ratio** in the drop-down menu. Notice how the guidelines within the crop area change. The view options help align and balance the elements of the image.

28. Click the **Commit Current Crop Operation** button (check mark) on the right-hand side of the **Options** bar. This executes the crop and removes all parts of the image covered by the red shield. Note: cropping changes the size of the canvas.

29. Click **Canvas Size...** in the **Image** pull-down menu. The **Canvas Size** dialog box is displayed, as shown in **Figure 4-3**.

30. Click in the **Width:** text box and enter 6. Make sure the drop-down arrow is set to **Inches**.

31. Click in the **Height:** text box and enter 10. Make sure the drop-down arrow is set to **Inches**.

32. In the **Anchor:** area, click the bottom-center box. The anchor is the point from where the operation will be applied. It is like putting a pin in the image at the

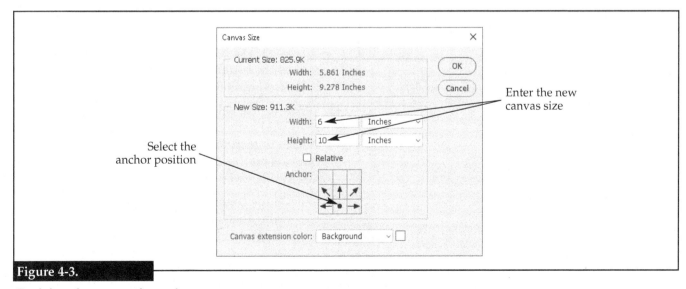

Figure 4-3.

Resizing the canvas for an image.

Quick Selection Tool

anchor point so when the canvas is made larger or smaller, the image stays pinned to that position.

33. Click the **OK** button to change the canvas size.

Isolating an Image Element

Most of the unwanted parts of the image have been cropped from the image. Now, the superhero character must be isolated from the background.

34. Click the **Quick Selection Tool** button on the **Tools** panel. The **Quick Selection Tool** allows you to click areas to be included in the selection. You can also click and hold to "paint" a selection area.

35. Click the **Select and Mask...** button on the **Options** bar. The Select and Mask workspace is set current. This is a special workspace containing tools and options for making and fine-tuning selections. Notice that the entire image is covered by a semitransparent overlay of white. Anything covered by this overlay will not be part of the selection, so right now nothing is selected. The level of transparency for the overlay is controlled by the **Transparency** slider in the **Properties** panel displayed on the right-hand side of the screen.

36. Click the **Quick Selection Tool** on the **Tools** panel. This tool is used to click areas to be included in the selection. You can also click and hold to "paint" a selection.

37. Click once in the middle of the superhero. Notice that the tool automatically selects an area that is the same color or has a border. The overlay is removed in this area.

38. Click and hold the mouse button, and push the selection area outward to try and include the entire hero as one selection. Clicking selects an area. Holding down the [Alt] key while clicking deselects an area. The selection does not have to be extremely close for this exercise, and the **Quick Selection Tool** works well for this purpose.

39. Right-click on the selected area, and click **Select Inverse** in the shortcut menu. This reverses what is selected with what is unselected. In other words, since the superhero is selected, this selects the background.

40. Click **Inverse** in the **Select** pull-down menu, which is another way to invert the selection. The previous selection is restored, which is the superhero.

41. On the **Options** bar, click the drop-down arrow, and in the drop-down menu, enter 10 in the **Size:** text box, as shown in **Figure 4-4**. This makes the brush smaller so the selection can be increased to include finer details.

42. Clean up the selection edge on your superhero if needed using this smaller brush. Use the **Add to Selection** and **Subtract from Selection** buttons on the **Options** bar as needed. These are alternatives to using the [Alt] key.

43. Click **Edge Detection** in the **Properties** panel to expand that area. If that area is already expanded, clicking **Edge Detection** collapses it.

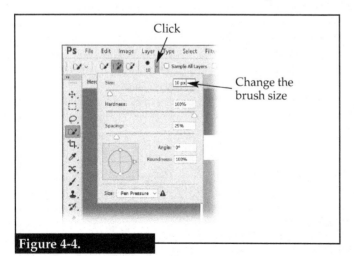

Figure 4-4.

Changing the size of a brush.

44. Click in the **Radius:** text box, and enter **60**. Notice how the white area blurs into the selection, which is indicated by removal of some of the color in the image.

45. Drag the **Radius:** slider to the left until the radius shown on the image is approximately the outline of the superhero character.

46. Drag the **Smooth:** slider to the right to a setting of 60 pixels (px). Notice that any sharp points on the image are rounded. Smoothing takes away any sharp angles and points. Return the setting to 0 pixels.

47. Drag the **Feather:** slider to the right to a setting of 10 pixels. Notice the edge has a uniform blur similar to the radius setting. Return the setting to 0 pixels.

48. Drag the **Contrast:** slider to the right to a setting of 60%. Notice the edge is sharply defined. Contrast adjusts the color balance on the image to make it stand out more from the background. Return the setting to 0%.

49. Drag the **Shift Edge:** slider to the right to a setting of +30%. This pushes the selection outward. A negative value will push the selection inward. When the selection is modified using the other settings, sometimes the defined edge is lost. The **Shift Edge** setting can help restore the selection edge.

50. Click the **OK** button at the bottom of the **Properties** panel. A layer mask is created, as indicated in the **Layers** panel. The Select and Mask workspace is also exited and the previous workspace (Essentials) is restored.

51. Right-click on the layer mask thumbnail in the **Layers** panel to display a shortcut menu. Examine the options in this menu.

52. Click **Add Mask to Selection** in the shortcut menu. If there were a current selection, the mask would be added to that selection, but since nothing is selected, the mask becomes the selected area.

TIP

The [Delete] key can be used to remove the selected area.

53. Right-click on the mask thumbnail again, and click **Apply Layer Mask** in the shortcut menu. Anything on the layer that was covered by the mask is deleted. Notice that the selection made from the mask is still active.

Creating a Layer from a Selection

54. Applying what you have learned, cancel the selection.

55. Applying what you have learned, select just the character's right hand.

56. Right-click on the selection, and click **Layer Via Cut** in the shortcut menu. This cuts the selected area from the Layer 1 layer and places it on a new layer. No change is visible in the image as the layers are stacked, but Layer 2 now appears in the **Layers** panel.

57. Applying what you have learned, turn off the visibility of Layer 2. The right hand is no longer visible. The hand is still part of the image, just not visible because the layer it is on has been hidden.

58. Applying what you have learned, turn on the visibility of Layer 2. The hand is visible again.

Applying Layer Styles and Effects

59. Click Layer 1 in the **Layers** panel to make it the current layer. This is the layer containing the character minus the hand.

fx

Add a Layer Style

60. Click the **Add a Layer Style** button (fx) at the bottom of the **Layers** panel to display a menu. The commands in this menu apply effects to the current layer.

61. Click **Stroke...** in the drop-down menu. The **Layer Style** dialog box is displayed with **Stroke** automatically checked and selected, as shown in **Figure 4-5.** Stroke is another word for line or shape outline.

62. Click in the **Size:** text box, and enter 7. This is the width of the stroke in pixels.

63. Click the **Color:** swatch to open a color picker dialog box. Notice the color can be defined using any of the five color models. Change the color to light blue by entering 0 in the **R:** text box, 225 in the **G:** text box, and 255 in the **B:** text box. Then, close the color picker.

64. Click the **OK** button to close the **Layer Style** dialog box and apply the stroke. The character is outlined in blue, except for the right hand. The style is applied to the layer, not the entire image. If any of the stroke appears to be applied to the hand, it is because small areas around the hand remained in Layer 1 when the hand was moved to Layer 2.

Adding to the Image

65. Click the **Ellipse Tool** in the **Tools** panel.

66. Click anywhere on the canvas and drag to draw an oval about 2" tall and 2.5" wide. As you drag, the dimensions of the object are displayed as help text. Notice the object is added to a new layer named Ellipse 1.

67. Double-click the thumbnail for the Ellipse 1 layer in the **Layers** panel. The **Color Picker** dialog box is displayed.

68. Applying what you have learned, create a color with hue of 250, saturation of 80%, and brightness of 100%. Close the color picker. The color of the ellipse is changed.

69. Applying what you have learned, move the ellipse shape so it covers the superhero's head.

Ellipse Tool

TIP
Rulers can be displayed along the sides of the document by clicking **Rulers** in the **View** pull-down menu.

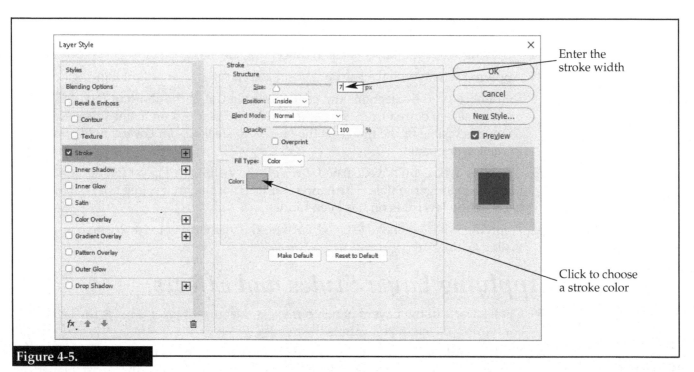

Figure 4-5.

Applying a stroke to a layer.

70. In the **Layers** panel, click and hold the Ellipse 1 layer, drag it to the bottom of the layer stack above Background, and drop it. This rearranges the layers so the Ellipse 1 layer is on the bottom. Any content on layers above it will hide parts of the ellipse. The result is the ellipse simulates a halo effect behind the superhero's head.

Rounded Rectangle Tool

71. Click the **Rounded Rectangle Tool** in the **Tools** panel, and draw a shape centered at the top of the canvas to fit above the superhero's head. It can overlap the ellipse.

72. Applying what you have learned, change the color of the rounded rectangle to yellow.

Horizontal Type Tool

73. Click the **Horizontal Type Tool** button in the **Tools** panel. Notice the **Options** bar displays common property settings for text, such as typeface, style, size, alignment, and color.

74. Click anywhere on the canvas and drag to create a text box. By creating a text box, the text will be paragraph text. If you just single-click, the text will be single-line text (not a paragraph).

75. Enter the text My Superhero in the text box. Notice the text is placed on a new layer.

Toggle the Character and Paragraph Panels

76. Click the **Toggle the Character and Paragraph Panels** button in the **Options** bar. This will open the panel group containing the **Character** and **Paragraph** panels. These panels can be used to set various options for text.

77. Display the **Paragraph** panel, and then click the **Justify all** button. Justification is a typesetting term that describes how the lines of type are set. To *justify* lines of text is to adjust the spacing between words so the beginning and end of each line is aligned to the left and right margins. Notice how the space between My and Superhero is increased, and My aligns with the left margin and Superhero aligns with the right margin. Examine the icons on the four justification buttons to see a representation of how these options affect the text.

78. Click the **Center text** button on the **Paragraph** panel. Justification is removed from the text, and the text is aligned to the center of the text box.

79. Applying what you have learned, move the text so it is centered on the yellow rectangle.

80. In the **Layers** panel, click the text layer, hold the [Ctrl] key, and click the Rounded Rectangle 1 layer. This selects both layers.

Link Layers

81. Click the **Link Layers** button at the bottom of the **Layers** panel. These two layers are now *linked,* or locked together, as indicated by the chain icon to the right of the layer names, as shown in **Figure 4-6.** Moving one layer automatically moves the other layer, so the text and yellow rectangle can be moved as one.

Polygon Tool

82. Applying what you have learned, use the **Polygon Tool** to add a green, five-sided polygon on the left side of the canvas.

83. With the Polygon 1 layer selected in the **Layers** panel, click **Layer>Rasterize>Layer** in the **Menu** bar. This converts the shape layer to a raster layer that defines each pixel of the image layer. You will no longer be able to change the color of the shape by double-clicking on its layer in the **Layers** panel. Notice the thumbnail has changed from showing just the polygon to showing the entire canvas with the polygon in place.

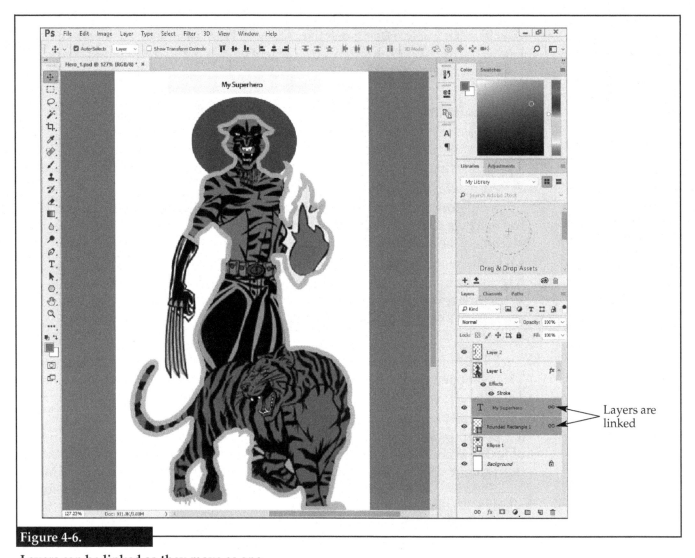

Figure 4-6.

Layers can be linked so they move as one.

Magic Wand Tool

Gradient Tool

84. Click the **Magic Wand Tool** in the **Tools** panel, and click anywhere inside the green polygon. The magic wand selects all adjacent pixels of the same color as the pixel clicked, so the entire green polygon is selected.

85. Click in the **Tolerance:** text box in the **Options** bar, and change the tolerance to 0. The tolerance setting determines how close of a match the adjacent color needs to be to be included in the magic wand selection. A tolerance of 0 requires all adjacent pixels to be the same color. A tolerance of 100 allows adjacent pixels of vastly different colors to be selected. Since the polygon is a single color, a tolerance of 0 can be used.

86. Click the **Gradient Tool** in the **Tools** panel.

87. Applying what you have learned, display the **Swatches** panel.

88. Left-click on the red swatch to set the foreground color. Notice in the **Options** bar that red is the first color of the gradient, as shown in **Figure 4-7.** Also notice the current background color is the second color of the gradient.

89. Click the drop-down arrow next to the gradient sample in the **Options** bar. The drop-down menu displayed contains several preset gradient styles. Hover the cursor over each style to display the name of the preset as help text.

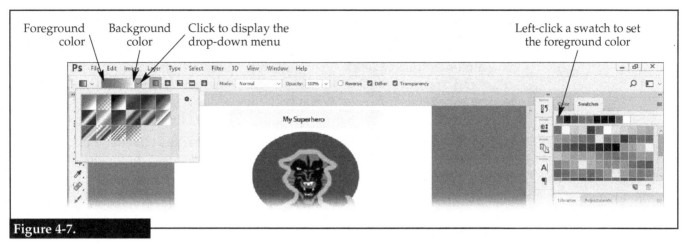

Figure 4-7.

Defining a gradient.

Linear Gradient

TIP
If a selection is active, the gradient is limited to the selection. If no selection is active, the gradient is applied to the entire layer.

Create a new Levels adjustment layer

90. Click the Transparent Rainbow style in the drop-down menu. Notice how the gradient preview changes to match the style. Click the drop-down button or press the [Esc] key to close the menu.

91. To the right of the gradient preview on the **Options** bar are commands to control how the gradient is applied. Click the **Linear Gradient** button.

92. Click near the bottom of the selection (the polygon), drag toward the top, and release to draw a *gradient line.* The gradient is drawn following the gradient line. Notice that since the two outside colors of the gradient are transparent, the original green color of the polygon may still be seen outside of the gradient.

Adjusting the Image

93. Click the **Collapse to Icons** button (>>) at the top of the panels to make the canvas area larger.

94. Applying what you have learned, expand the collapsed **Adjustments** panel.

95. Click the **Create a new Levels adjustments layer** button. The **Properties** panel is displayed containing a histogram that illustrates the color density of each color channel. A *histogram* is a chart showing the frequency of occurrence, so the higher the line the higher the color density.

96. Click the drop-down arrow above the histogram, and click **Green** in the drop-down list, as shown in **Figure 4-8.** Only the green channel is displayed in the histogram.

97. At the bottom of the histogram are three sliders for adjusting the color saturation: shadows, midtones, and highlights. Click the shadows slider, which is the left-hand slider, and drag it to the right. Notice how the colors in the gradient become darker. The green colors become nearly black the farther to the right you drag the slider. The other colors are not affected as much because only the green channel is displayed in the histogram.

Click to select the channel

Histogram

Saturation sliders

Brightness sliders

Figure 4-8.

Adjusting color levels.

98. Below the histogram is a gradient bar containing two sliders to adjust the color brightness. The left-hand slider is the input for pure black, and the right-hand slider is the input for pure white. The position of the sliders on the bar determines the output level. Click the white slider, which is the right-hand slider, and drag it to the left. Notice how much darker the colors of the rainbow become as white is removed. When the white slider is in the middle of the bar, pure white is replaced with gray, which is why the colors become darker.

99. Applying what you have learned, collapse the **Properties** panel and expand the **History** panel. Notice a list of different *states,* or stages, of the document is shown. Up to 20 states are stored in the default history panel list.

100. Select the last state in the **History** panel (Gradient) by checking the box to the left of the state. This action sets which state will be used as the source for the history brush.

101. Click the **Create a new snapshot** button at the bottom of the **History** panel. A *snapshot* is a duplicate of the working image in its current form. This is similar to saving the image using a different file name to create a copy of the image, except the snapshot is not saved. Snapshots are cleared when the file is closed or Photoshop is exited. However, snapshots are ideal for seeing the before and after of changes such as applying an image filter.

102. Right-click on the last history state, and click **Delete** in the shortcut menu. In the dialog box that appears asking if you want to delete the state, click the **Yes** button. The state is removed, and the image is restored to its previous state. In effect, the color alterations to the gradient are undone. Note: states must be removed in order from the bottom up.

103. Applying what you have learned, close the **History** panel, expand the normally expanded panels, and select the layer that contains the yellow rectangle.

104. Display the **Adjustments** panel, and click the **Create a new Black & White adjustment layer** button. The **Properties** panel is displayed containing settings for removing color, as shown in **Figure 4-9**. Note: using the **Adjustments** panel applies nondestructive editing.

105. Collapse the **Properties** panel to accept the default settings. Notice that a new layer is created above the layer containing the yellow rectangle, and all layers below this new layer have the color removed.

Managing Layers

106. In the **Layers** panel, drag the Ellipse 1 layer above the Black & White 1 layer. Notice how color is restored to the ellipse.

107. Click the **Create a new group** button in the **Layers** panel. A group is added to the layer stack above the current layer. A *group* is a folder into which layers can be placed, which can help to better organize a project.

TIP

The **History** panel can be resized by dragging the lower-right corner of the panel.

Create a new snapshot

Create a new Black & White adjustment layer

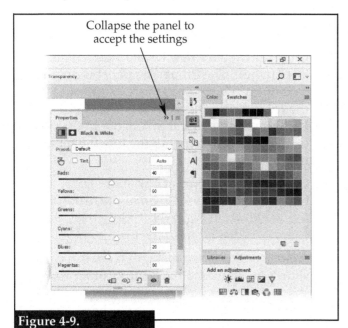

Collapse the panel to accept the settings

Figure 4-9.

Creating a layer to remove color.

Create a new group

108. Double-click on the Group 1 name. The name appears in a text box. Enter the new name of Nonhero Layers.

109. Right-click on the Nonhero Layers group, and click **Red** in the shortcut menu. A red background is added for the group in the **Layers** panel. This is only for organizational purposes and does not affect the image.

110. Hold down the [Ctrl] key, and click each layer in the **Layers** panel that does not contain part of the superhero image. The [Ctrl] key allows you to select multiple individual layers. Do not select the Nonhero Layers group or the Background layer.

111. Drag the selected layers, and drop them into the group. The selected layers are moved into the group folder, which is indicated by the red background that now appears in the **Layers** panel for each of those layers.

112. Click the triangle next to the folder icon in the Nonhero Layers group. The group is closed or collapsed, and all of the layers it contains are hidden in the **Layers** panel. However, the layers are still visible in the document.

113. Click the triangle again to display the layers within the Nonhero Layers group.

114. Applying what you have learned, change the name of the layer containing the rounded rectangle to Title Block.

Managing the Workspace

As you have seen, it is easy to move panels. After you gain experience with Photoshop, you may want to rearrange the panels to configure the workspace to better match how you work. After you have the workspace adjusted to suit your preferences, the workspace can be saved.

115. Click the workspace switcher button, and click **Reset Essentials** in the drop-down menu. This ensures any modifications you have made to the workspace are undone.

116. Click **View>Rulers** in the **Menu** bar. Rulers are displayed along the top and left-hand side of the work area. The units displayed in the ruler are inches by default.

117. Right-click on either ruler, and click **Centimeters** in the shortcut menu. The units for both rulers are changed to centimeters.

118. Applying what you have learned, drag the **Color** panel, and drop it below the **Layers** panel. Notice that only the **Color** panel is moved even though it had been grouped with the **Swatches** panel.

119. Reset the workspace to default.

120. Look at the group of the **Color** panel and the **Swatches** panel. There is a blank space to the right of the panel names, as shown in **Figure 4-10.** Click and hold on the blank space, and drag the panel group below the **Layers** panel. The entire panel group is moved, not just a single panel. When the group is over the bottom of the **Layers** panel, a blue line appears. Drop the panel group when this line appears and the panel group snaps into place. The process of moving a panel or group so it snaps in place is called *docking.*

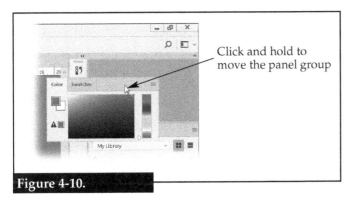

Click and hold to move the panel group

Figure 4-10.

Relocating a panel.

121. Applying what you have learned, dock the **Layers** panel group as the last panel group, and dock the **History** panel above the **Layers** panel group.

122. Move the **Libraries** panel into the **Color** panel group.

123. To save this workspace configuration, click the workspace switcher, and click **New Workspace...** in the drop-down menu. The **New Workspace** dialog box is displayed, as shown in **Figure 4-11**.

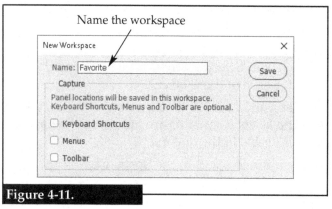

Figure 4-11.

Saving a new workspace.

124. Click in the **Name:** text box, and enter Favorite, and click the **Save** button. The workspace switcher now displays the name **Favorite**.

125. Applying what you have learned, restore the Essentials workspace and reset it. Make note of the panel locations. Notice the rulers still display centimeters as the units. The ruler setting is not saved in the workspace. Continue to use this workspace for the remainder of the lessons.

126. Applying what you have learned, set the rulers to display inches. Leave the rulers displayed for the remainder of the lessons.

127. Save the file, and close Photoshop.

Lesson Review

Vocabulary

In a word processing document or on a sheet of paper, list all of the *key terms* in this lesson. Place each term on a separate line. Then, write a definition for each term using your own words. You will continue to build this terminology dictionary throughout this certification guide.

Review Questions

Answer the following questions. These questions are aligned to questions in the certification exam. Answering these questions will help prepare you to take the exam.

1. How can the canvas be resized only to the right-hand side?

_____

_____

2. List two ways to invert the selection.

_____

_____

3. Describe how to remove a selected area from an image.

_____

_____

4. Describe the function of the **Layer Via Cut** tool.

_____

_____

5. Where is the **Add a Layer Style** tool located?

_____

6. Which layer style applies an outline color to the image elements on the layer?

_____

7. How can a layer be moved below another layer?

_____

_____

8. Describe how to change the color of a drawn shape, such as an ellipse.

_____

_____

9. How is a new horizontal type layer added?

_____

10. What happens when a shape layer is rasterized?

_____

_____

11. Which tool is used to select an area with the same color with only a single click?

_____

12. List the steps needed to apply a gradient to a selection using the current foreground and background colors.

_____

_____

_____

_____

13. Where is the command located that will create a new layer group?

_____

14. Describe how to save the layout of the panels and toolbar.

_____

_____

15. Which tool creates a selection by painting over an area of the image?

_____

16. List the steps needed to rotate one layer of an image 90 degrees counterclockwise.

_____

_____

17. If paragraph text is justified to the right, what is the effect?

_____

_____

18. A designer wants to select a section of the blue sky in a photograph using the **Magic Wand Tool**. When the sky is clicked, only part of the blue sky is selected. What needs to be done so the tool will select the entire sky with one click?

_____

_____

19. What feature of Photoshop can be used to compare the before and after of applying a filter to an image?

_____

20. Describe how to display the rulers and to change the unit of measurement from inches to pixels.

_____

_____

_____

_____

Lesson 5
Destructive and Nondestructive Editing

Objectives

Students will isolate an image element. Students will save a selection. Students will apply a nondestructive layer mask. Students will use zoom tools. Students will explain how to use the **Spot Healing Brush Tool**. Students will flatten an image. Students will explain smart filters. Students will describe an unsharp mask.

Situation

The Nocturnal Interactive Computer Entertainment (NICE) company wants you to create a new image for the superhero created in the previous lesson. The new image will be photo based. The first step is to edit a portrait photograph to create an image of just the person's face. This file will be used later to create the final image, so quality of work is an important attribute for this project. You will also gain valuable experience that will help you prepare for certification.

How to Begin

1. Before beginning this lesson, download the needed files from the student companion website located at www.g-wlearning.com, and unzip them into your working folder.

2. Launch Photoshop.

3. Applying what you have learned, begin a new project named *LastName_TigerMan_1* with an 8″ × 10″ white background in the RGB color model at an 8 bit, 72 pixel density.

4. Save the document as *LastName_TigerMan_1* in your working folder.

TIP
To keep the placed image proportional, hold down the [Shift] key while dragging the handles.

Isolating an Image Element

5. Applying what you have learned, place (embed) the Face image file.

6. Drag the corner handles of the placed image so the image fills the entire canvas, as shown in **Figure 5-1.** Press the [Enter] key to accept the placement.

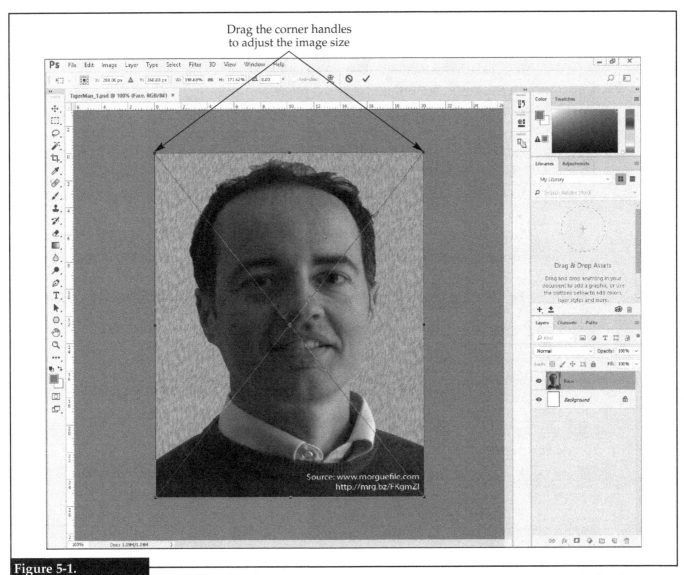

Figure 5-1.

Adjusting the size of a placed image.

**Magnetic
Lasso Tool**

7. Click the **Magnetic Lasso Tool** button in the **Tools** panel. This tool creates a selection by snapping to areas where color changes as you drag an outline.

8. Click near the edge of the face, and carefully trace the outline of the face and the hair. To end the outline and create the selection, click the beginning anchor point. If the outline gets too far from the face, press the [Esc] key to cancel the tool, and start over.

9. Applying what you have learned, use the **Quick Select Tool** to clean up the selection as needed.

Saving a Selection

The ability to save a selection is a powerful feature. Later, the saved selection can be reloaded or loaded on to a different image, which can save a lot of time over creating the selection again.

10. Click **Save Selection...** in the **Select** pull-down menu. The **Save Selection** dialog box is displayed, as shown in **Figure 5-2**.

11. Make sure the **Document:** drop-down arrow is set to the current document (TigerMan_1) and the **Channel:** drop-down arrow is set to **New**. These settings will embed the saved selection with this document and display it on the **Channels** panel.

12. Click in the **Name:** text box, and enter Face Selection.

13. Click the **OK** button to save the selection.

14. Click the **Channels** panel in the **Layers** panel group. Notice the Face Selection is displayed as a mask in the panel, as shown in **Figure 5-3**. The white area of the mask is the selected area and the black area is not contained in the selection.

15. Click **Deselect** in the **Select** pull-down menu.

16. Click **Load Selection...** in the **Select** pull-down menu. The **Load Selection** dialog box is displayed.

17. Make sure the **Document:** drop-down arrow displays the TigerMan_1 document.

18. Click the **Channel:** drop-down arrow, and click **Face Selection** in the drop-down menu.

19. Click the **OK** button. The face is reselected as the saved selection is loaded.

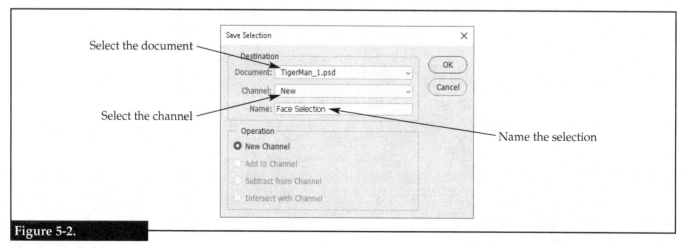

Figure 5-2.

Saving a selection.

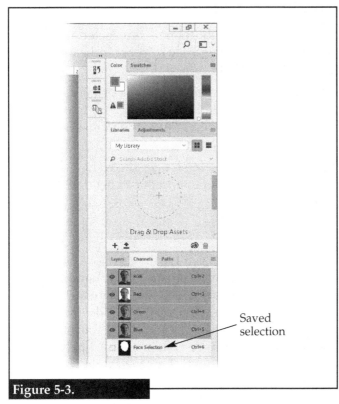

Figure 5-3.

A selection is displayed as a mask in the **Layers** panel.

Nondestructive Layer Mask

Remember that the Face Selection is displayed as a mask in the **Channels** panel. If this mask is applied to the image, the black area will be hidden.

20. Applying what you have learned, rename the current layer as Face Isolated.

21. Click the **Add Layer Mask** button at the bottom of the **Layers** panel. A nondestructive layer mask is applied to the image. *Nondestructive editing* involves making changes that do not permanently eliminate the original image data. Notice the layer and mask are linked.

22. Right-click on the mask thumbnail in the **Layers** panel, and click **Disable Layer Mask** in the shortcut menu. The area hidden by the mask is restored. This is possible because the layer mask is nondestructive.

23. Right-click on the mask thumbnail in the **Layers** panel, and click **Enable Layer Mask** in the shortcut menu. The face is again isolated.

Zooming In and Out

24. Click in the zoom setting text box at the lower-left corner of the workspace, and enter 40. When the [Enter] key is pressed, the view of the document is reduced to 40% of actual size.

25. Click the **Zoom Tool** button on the **Tools** panel.

26. Click and drag a box around the face. The view of the document is zoomed in to the selected area.

27. Press the [Alt] key and click once on the canvas. The view of the document is zoomed out. Continue zooming out until the document fills the view.

Spot Healing

The **Spot Healing Brush Tool** blends the color of adjacent pixels. This tool allows the designer to paint over a small imperfection on the image to repair or "heal" the area. This is often done to remove dust specks from a scanned image.

28. Applying what you have learned, cancel the selection and zoom in on the area above the left eyebrow.

29. Click the **Spot Healing Brush Tool** button in the **Tools** panel.

30. Applying what you have learned, use the **Options** bar to change the brush size to 10 pixels.

31. With the drop-down menu still displayed, click in the **Hardness:** text box, and enter 15. This setting will produce soft edges on the brush and make it easier to blend away any blemishes.

Saved selection

Add Layer Mask

Zoom Tool

TIP

A shortcut for zooming in is pressing the [Ctrl] key and the space bar at the same time. This can be activated within another tool.

Spot Healing Brush Tool

32. Press the [Enter] key to accept the settings in the drop-down menu.

33. Make sure the image thumbnail, not the mask thumbnail, is selected in the **Layers** panel, and then click on the pimple. A message appears indicating the smart object must be rasterized. Click the **OK** button.

34. After the layer is rasterized, click on the pimple, and move the brush around. As you paint, the area that will be affected is highlighted in black. Try to paint over as little as possible to get the best blend. When you release the mouse button, the highlighted area is "healed."

35. Applying what you have learned, remove the blemish near the right eyebrow and the mole on the left side of the mouth. Zoom in and out as needed. When finished, zoom the image to fill the screen.

Flattening an Image

To the right of the zoom setting text box is a display of settings information. By default, the settings information displays the document file size. There are either one or two numbers. If one number is displayed, it is the size of the file. If two numbers are displayed, the second number is the size of the file in its current state, and the first number would be the file size if the image is flattened. A *flattened* image has all of its layers collapsed into the background. This is *destructive editing* because there is no way to restore the original data, except by using the undo tool *immediately* after flattening the image or by using the **History** panel.

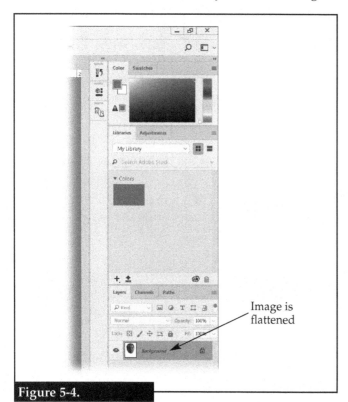

Image is flattened

Figure 5-4.

Flattening an image collapses all layers into a background layer.

Delete current state

36. Click the triangle button to the right of the settings information, and click **Current Tool** in the drop-down menu that is displayed. The name of the current tool is displayed in the settings information.

37. Click a different tool in the **Tools** panel, such as the **Move** tool. The settings information shows the name of the current tool.

38. Click the triangle button to the right of the settings information, and click **Document Sizes** in the drop-down menu. Make note of the two document file sizes.

39. Click **Layer>Flatten Image** in the **Menu** bar. This applies the layer mask and replaces the area masked out with the current background color, as shown in **Figure 5-4.**

40. Applying what you have learned, display the **History** panel.

41. Select the Flatten Image state, and click the **Delete current state** button at the bottom of the panel.

42. In the dialog box that appears asking if you want to delete the state, click the **Yes** button. The state is deleted and the image is no longer flattened.

43. Collapse the **History** panel.

Smart Filters

Filters can alter an image by adding or taking away elements. *Smart filters* are filters applied to a smart object. If the object is already converted to a smart object, any filter applied will be a smart filter.

TIP
Before applying a filter, it is always a best practice to convert the layer to a smart object, if it is not already, by clicking **Layer>Smart Objects>Convert to Smart Object**.

44. Click the **Filter** pull-down menu. Notice there are many types of filters.

45. Locate the **Convert for Smart Filters** command in the pull-down menu. This command prepares the image on the current layer to accept filters as smart filters. Using filters in smart-filter mode allows the filter to be adjusted at a later stage. Otherwise, the filter cannot be adjusted after it is applied.

46. Click **Convert for Smart Filters**. In the message that appears, click the **OK** button. The layer is converted to a smart object, and the mask is applied as a destructive edit. Any filters applied to the layer now will be smart filters.

47. Click **Filter>Sharpen>Sharpen Edges**. A sharpen edges filter is applied to the layer, which will make finer details in the image, such as the hair, clearer. Notice that the filter is a smart filter and appears in the **Layers** panel, as shown in **Figure 5-5**, because it is a nondestructive edit.

Unsharp Mask

48. Applying what you have learned, load the Face Selection saved selection.

49. Click **Filter>Sharpen>Unsharp Mask...** An unsharp mask can provide more control over the sharpening of the edges of a selection.

50. In the **Unsharp Mask** dialog box, click in the **Amount:** text box, and enter 100, as shown in **Figure 5-6**.

TIP
You can pan the preview by clicking and dragging the preview image.

51. Click in the **Radius:** text box, and enter 0.5.

52. Click in the **Threshold:** text box, and enter 1. Notice how the changes appear in the preview window.

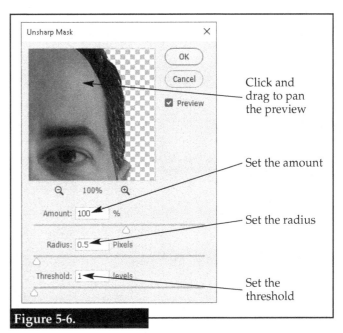

Figure 5-5.
Smart filters appear as a separate item in the **Layers** panel and can be adjusted at any time.

Figure 5-6.
Applying an unsharp mask.

53. Click the **OK** button to close the **Unsharp Mask** dialog box and apply the filter. This will sharpen the edges of the selection. This filter is also a smart filter.

54. Save the file, and close Photoshop.

Lesson Review

Vocabulary

In a word processing document or on a sheet of paper, list all of the *key terms* in this lesson. Place each term on a separate line. Then, write a definition for each term using your own words. You will continue to build this terminology dictionary throughout this certification guide.

Review Questions

Answer the following questions. These questions are aligned to questions in the certification exam. Answering these questions will help prepare you to take the exam.

1. Which selection tool snaps to color changes where the tool is used?

2. How is a saved selection placed back on an image?

3. Where is the command to add a nondestructive mask located?

4. What is the difference between nondestructive editing and destructive editing?

5. Where would a digital artist see the current document file size in Photoshop?

6. What happens when an image is flattened?

7. List two ways a layer can be converted into a smart object.

8. How is a filter applied as a smart filter?

9. What is the purpose of having a layer as a smart object?

_____

_____

10. How would a digital artist using Photoshop sharpen the edges of the selection by changing the radius of the selection?

_____

_____

Lesson 6
Working with Layers

Objectives

Students will remove red-eye from a photograph. Students will use different brush types. Students will apply the rule of thirds. Students will create text. Students will describe the purpose of a clipping mask. Students will explain copyright. Students will resize an image. Students will print an image to fit on the selected print media.

Situation

The Nocturnal Interactive Computer Entertainment (NICE) company needs large- and small-scale images of the tiger-themed series. You need to make edits to different Photoshop files and create items for each image. Make sure you properly save these images so they can be edited later.

How to Begin

1. Before beginning this lesson, download the needed files from the student companion website located at www.g-wlearning.com, and unzip them into your working folder.
2. Launch Photoshop.
3. Open the TigerMan_1 file created in the last lesson.

Removing Red-eye

Create a new layer

4. Click the **Create a new layer** button in the **Layers** panel. A new layer named Layer 1 is added. New layers are always named Layer n, where n is a sequential number.
5. Applying what you have learned, rename the new layer as Tiger.

Red Eye Tool

Hand Tool

TIP

The hand tool can be activated by pressing the space bar. This allows the image to be quickly panned while within another tool.

6. Applying what you have learned, place the file Red Eye Tiger onto the Tiger layer, and resize it to fit the canvas. Notice the name of the layer has changed to the name of the placed image file.

7. Change the layer name back to Tiger.

8. Applying what you have learned, turn off the visibility of the Face Isolated layer. This ensures no changes are accidentally made to the layer.

9. Click the **Red Eye Tool** in the **Tools** panel.

10. Applying what you have learned, zoom in on the left eye of the tiger (on the right side of the image).

11. Click on the red spot in the eye. If asked to rasterize the smart object, click the **OK** button.

12. Continue using the tool by dragging a rectangle that covers the entire red spot in the eye.

13. Repeat dragging a rectangle over the red spot until the spot is completely removed.

14. Click the **Hand Tool** in the **Tools** panel.

15. Click, hold, and drag to the right to pan the image to the left. *Panning* is sliding the image around in the view to see a different area.

16. Continue panning until the right eye is visible.

17. Applying what you have learned, remove the red spot from the right eye.

18. Applying what you have learned, zoom out to 100%.

19. Save the file. You will use the TigerMan_1 file in a later lesson.

20. Save the file as *LastName*_Tiger in your working folder. You will continue editing this image.

Brush Types

A *pixel mask* allows you to darken or erase parts of a layer so layers below it show through. Grayscale values control how much transparency is applied. You will use different brush types to paint the pixel mask to create blades of grass surrounding the tiger.

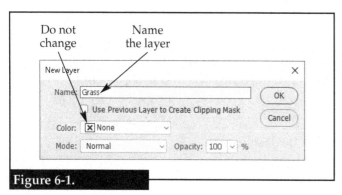

Figure 6-1.

Creating a new layer.

21. Click the foreground color swatch in the **Tools** panel. The color picker is displayed for setting the foreground color.

22. Set the foreground color to R70, G120, B30. This is a yellow-green. Close the color picker.

23. Click **New Fill Layer** and then **Solid Color...** from the **Layer** pull-down menu. The **New Layer** dialog box is displayed, as shown in **Figure 6-1**. A *fill layer* is a new layer that is completely covered in a fill, either a solid color, a gradient, or a pattern.

24. Click in the **Name:** text box, and enter Grass.

By default, the foreground color is added to any new shape or fill layer. It is best practice to change the foreground color prior to adding these elements.

Brush Tool

25. Click the **OK** button to accept the other default settings. The layer is created, and the **Color Picker** dialog box is displayed.

26. Click the **OK** button to close the color picker and accept the foreground color. Notice that the layer is created above whichever layer was current, so it is above the Tiger layer.

27. Applying what you have learned, move the Grass layer below the Tiger layer, and select the Tiger layer.

28. Applying what you have learned, add a layer mask to the Tiger layer.

29. Make sure the layer mask is selected, which is indicated by the dashed line around the thumbnail in the **Layers** panel, as shown in **Figure 6-2.** Look at the **Color** panel, and notice how the two swatches display black and white. Painting in black acts like an eraser to hide the layer. Painting in a shade of gray makes the area semitransparent. Painting in white makes the area fully opaque, or fully visible. In this case, you will be creating blades of grass, so the green layer below needs to show through. This means you need to paint in black.

30. If necessary, click the **Switch Foreground and Background Colors** arrow in the **Tools** panel so the black color swatch is on top (foreground color). This also swaps the colors in the **Color** panel.

31. Click the **Brush Tool** in the **Tools** panel.

32. On the **Options** bar, click the **Brush Preset Picker** drop-down arrow. In the drop-down menu that is displayed, click in the **Size:** text box, and enter 20, as shown in **Figure 6-3.** This sets the diameter of the brush.

33. Click anywhere on the image, and draw a squiggle mark across the tiger. Notice how the layer below the Tiger layer, which is the Grass layer, is fully revealed where the brush paints.

34. Click the **Brush Preset Picker** drop-down arrow, and change the **Hardness:** setting to 100%.

35. Draw another line anywhere on the image. Notice how the hardness of 100% has a crisp edge, whereas the previous line has a soft or feathered edge. *Hardness* controls the sharpness of a brush's edge.

36. Applying what you have learned, undo *both* brush actions.

Click to swap foreground and background colors

Dashed line indicates the mask is selected

Source: public domain

Figure 6-2.

Setting the mask color.

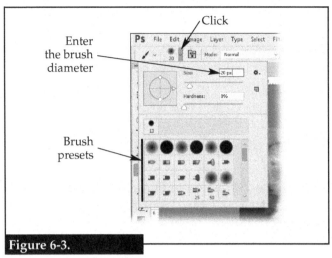

Figure 6-3.

Setting the brush size.

TIP
Notice the leaves brushes cannot have a hardness setting applied. Not every brush has this setting available.

37. Click the foreground color swatch, either in the **Tools** panel or the **Color** panel. In the color picker that is displayed, change the color to R150, G150, B150. This is a medium-gray.

38. Draw another squiggle mark on the tiger. Notice how the layer below is only partially visible. The shade of gray creates a semitransparent area, so part of the tiger remains visible.

39. Applying what you have learned, undo the brush action.

40. Applying what you have learned, change the foreground color to pure black (R0, G0, B0).

41. On the **Options** bar, click the **Brush Preset Picker** drop-down arrow. In the drop-down menu that is displayed, click the Grass 134 brush type in the list of presets.

42. Click and drag across the bottom of the image, just below the tiger's chin.

43. Continue to paint across the bottom of the image until most of the area below the tiger's chin is filled with grass.

44. Applying what you have learned, change the brush to Scattered Leaves 95, and set the foreground color to light gray (such as R190, G190, B190).

45. Paint along the top and sides of the tiger. The leaves will be semitransparent, so they will be subtle.

Rule of Thirds

Notice how these additions help focus attention on the tiger's face and his eyes. The eyes have always been a focus point due to the rule of thirds, as shown in **Figure 6-4.** Notice how the lines divide the tiger image into nine sections. The

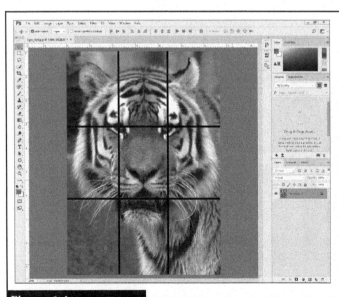
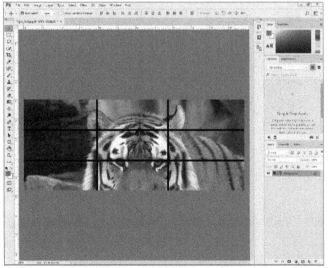

Figure 6-4.

The rule of thirds applied to two different crops of the same image. Notice how the focus shifts.

natural focal points are where the lines intersect. If the image is cropped, the focal points change, and the tiger's ears are where the viewer's eyes are naturally drawn. In the second image, the viewer may be led to think the tiger has just heard a noise and is focusing its attention on the sound. The rule of thirds is commonly used in graphic design and photography to compose a scene. In Photoshop, guidelines can be used to show the rule of thirds.

Move Tool

46. Click **New Guide…** in the **View** pull-down menu. The **New Guide** dialog box is displayed.

47. Click the **Horizontal** radio button, click in the **Position:** text box and enter 3.33 in, and click the **OK** button. A horizontal guideline is added to the document at the position specified.

48. Applying what you have learned, add another horizontal guideline at 6.67 inches and vertical guidelines at 2.67 inches and 5.33 inches. The four guidelines represent the rule of thirds on the current 8″ × 10″ document. Notice how the guidelines intersect at the tiger's eyes.

49. Click the **Move Tool** in the **Tools** panel.

50. Drag the Tiger layer around the canvas. Notice how your eye is always drawn to the intersections of the guidelines.

51. Click **Clear Guides** in the **View** pull-down menu to remove the guidelines. Notice how your eye is still drawn to where the guides intersected even though they are no longer displayed.

52. Applying what you have learned, undo moving the Tiger layer and adding the guides.

Creating Text

53. In the **Layers** panel, double-click on the thumbnail for the Grass layer (the green).

54. In the color picker, enter the color H23, S90, B51, and click the **OK** button. Notice how the new fill color is similar to the color of the tiger's fur. These are analogous colors, which do not provide contrast. The fill color has no contrast with the tiger's fur, so the leaves effect (pixel mask) across the top of the image seems to disappear. On the other hand, the grass effect (pixel mask) across the bottom of the image stands out against the white fur because white and the fill color are contrasting colors.

Horizontal Type Tool

Toggle the Character and Paragraph panels

55. Click the **Horizontal Type Tool** in the **Tools** panel.

56. Click above the tiger's head, and add the text The World of Tigers.

57. Applying what you have learned, move the text layer above the Tiger layer.

58. Activate the **Horizontal Type Tool**, and select the text just added by clicking at the beginning of the text, holding, and dragging to the end of the text.

59. Click the **Toggle the Character and Paragraph panels** button on the **Options** bar. The **Character** panel is displayed, as shown in **Figure 6-5.**

60. In the **Character** panel, click the **Search for and select fonts** drop-down arrow, and click a sans serif font in the drop-down list, such as Arial. Recall, sans serif fonts are traditionally used where legibility is important, such as a headline.

61. Click the **Set the font style** drop-down arrow, and click **Black** in the drop-down list. Black typeface is heavier than bold typeface. It has nothing to do with the

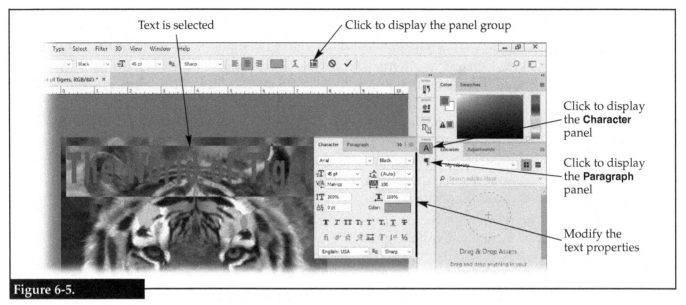

Text is selected   Click to display the panel group

Click to display the **Character** panel

Click to display the **Paragraph** panel

Modify the text properties

Figure 6-5.

The **Character** panel is used to modify the appearance of text.

color of the type. If black is not an option for the font family you selected, select bold or italic.

62. Click in the **Set the font size** text box, and enter 45.

63. Click in the **Set the kerning between two characters** text box, and enter 0. *Kerning* is the spacing between certain letters when they are adjacent to each other, such as A and V.

64. Click in the **Set the tracking for the selected characters** text box, and enter 100. *Tracking* is the overall spacing between all letters.

65. Click in the **Vertically Scale** text box, and enter 200%. This stretches the text in the vertical direction.

66. Click the color swatch, and in the color picker, use the CMYK color model to choose a medium or light blue, which is a complementary color to the color of the tiger's fur and will contrast with it. Close the color picker, and then collapse the **Character** panel.

Create warped text

67. With the text selected, click the **Create warped text** button on the **Options** bar. The **Warp Text** dialog box is displayed, as shown in **Figure 6-6**.

68. Click the **Style:** drop-down arrow, and click **Bulge** in the drop-down menu.

69. Drag the **Bend:** slider to the left to reduce the amount of the bulge, and then click the **OK** button to apply the effect.

70. Applying what you have learned, move the text so it is centered at the top of the image.

Clipping Mask

A *clipping mask* uses the content of a layer underneath the mask to block the layers above it. This is particularly useful when working with text. A texture layer below can be used to create the effect of filling the text with a texture.

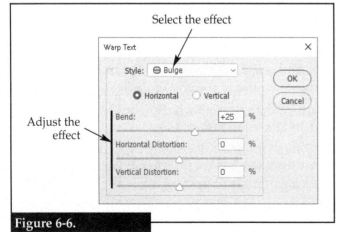

Select the effect

Adjust the effect

Figure 6-6.

Applying an effect to text.

71. Applying what you have learned, hide all of the layers except the text layer.

72. Applying what you have learned, create a new layer, and place it below the text layer.

73. Applying what you have learned, place the image of the tiger on the new layer. Move and size the image so fur is completely behind the text. The image will be larger than the canvas.

74. Rename the layer as Text Fill.

75. Move the Text Fill layer to the top of the layer stack. The text layer should be the second layer in the stack.

76. Select the Text Fill layer, and then click the panel menu button on the **Layers** panel. Click **Create Clipping Mask** in the menu. The fill color of the text is tiger fur, as shown in **Figure 6-7.** In effect, the text is acting like a cookie cutter to cut out part of the Text Fill layer. Notice the Text Fill layer has a downward arrow and icon in the **Layers** panel to indicate it is a clipping mask for the layer directly below it.

77. Select the text layer.

78. Use the **Move Tool** to drag the image around. Notice how the part cut out by the text changes, but the text does not move around. You are actually moving the

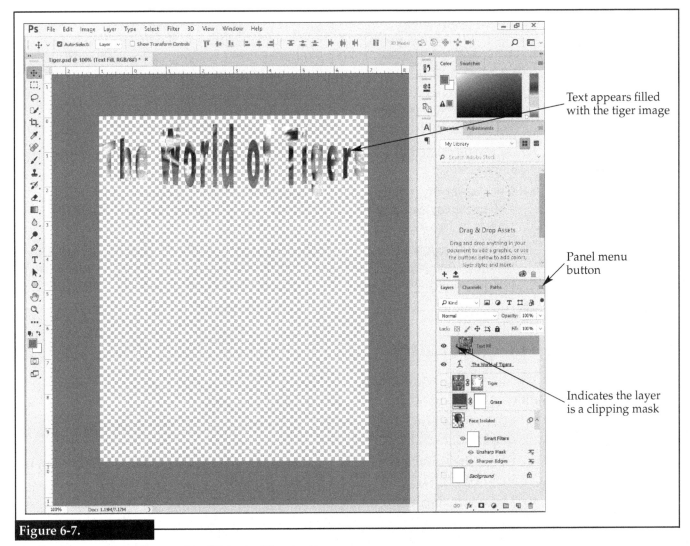

Text appears filled with the tiger image

Panel menu button

Indicates the layer is a clipping mask

Figure 6-7.

A clipping mask can be used to fill text with a texture.

clipping mask (the tiger image), not the text on the layer. Normally, when you use the **Move Tool** on a layer, the content of that layer is moved. In this case, the image used as the clipping mask is moved.

79. Make the Tiger and Grass layers visible.

80. Applying what you have learned, move the tiger image around until you are satisfied with the section of the image showing through the text. For example, you may find centering the tiger's whiskers in the text provides the best contrast so the text is readable.

81. Applying what you have learned, flatten the image. When prompted, discard any hidden layers.

Copyrights

According to the *World Intellectual Property Organization (WIPO) Copyright Treaty,* intellectual property, such as music, games, movies, and works of art, are protected worldwide. In the United States, the Digital Millennium Copyright Act (DCMA) enforces the WIPO treaty. Once an image or other intellectual property is produced in some tangible form, it is automatically copyrighted. A *copyright* is legal ownership of the work. However, some people may choose to break the law and violate the copyright by copying an image. A common tactic used to protect images is a watermark. A *watermark* is a design or symbol placed on the image to render it unusable, but so that somebody can still view the image. Often, the watermark is semitransparent. This forces somebody wanting to use the image to purchase it or otherwise obtain permission from the copyright holder to use it.

82. Applying what you have learned, add horizontal sans serif text that states Copyright Protected, size it to 45 points, set kerning of 0, set tracking of 0, set vertical scale of 100%, and change its color to white.

83. Applying what you have learned, move the text so it is across the middle of the tiger's face.

84. Click **Layer Style** and then **Blending Options...** in the **Layer** pull-down menu. The **Layer Style** dialog box is displayed with **Blending Options** selected, as shown in **Figure 6-8.**

85. Click in the **Opacity:** text box, enter 50%, and click the **OK** button. The layer is now 50% opaque, so the text appears ghosted. The main image can still be seen, but the watermark prevents it from being used for final artwork.

86. Applying what you have learned, flatten the image and save the file.

Image Sizing

The tiger image is going to be used on a website. It will be placed on the site as a thumbnail image, so the image size must be changed.

87. Click **Image Size...** in the **Image** pull-down menu. The **Image Size** dialog box is displayed, as shown in **Figure 6-9.**

88. Check the **Resample Image:** check box, and click **Bicubic Sharper (reduction)** in the corresponding drop-down menu.

89. Make sure the link icon between the width and height is on (depressed or dark gray). This locks the width and height settings so the aspect ratio does not change.

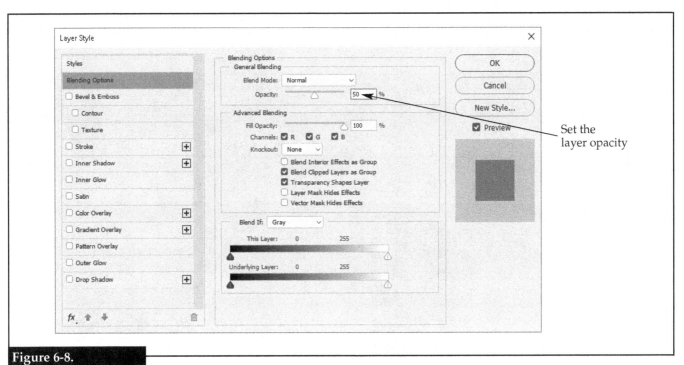

Set the
layer opacity

Figure 6-8.

Adjusting layer opacity.

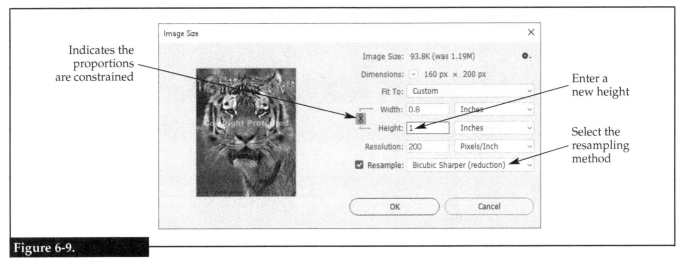

Indicates the
proportions
are constrained

Enter a
new height

Select the
resampling
method

Figure 6-9.

Resizing an image.

90. Click in the **Height:** text box in the **Document Size:** area, and enter 1. Make sure the corresponding drop-down menu is set to **Inches**. The setting in the **Width:** text box is automatically changed to 0.8 because the proportions are constrained.

91. Applying what you have learned, set the resolution to 200 pixels per inch. Then, click the **OK** button to change the image size. Notice how the image is much smaller.

92. Click **Export>Save for Web (Legacy)...** in the **File** pull-down menu. The **Save for Web** dialog box is displayed, as shown in **Figure 6-10.** Note: if you receive an error message that the system cannot find the path specified, skip to the next section.

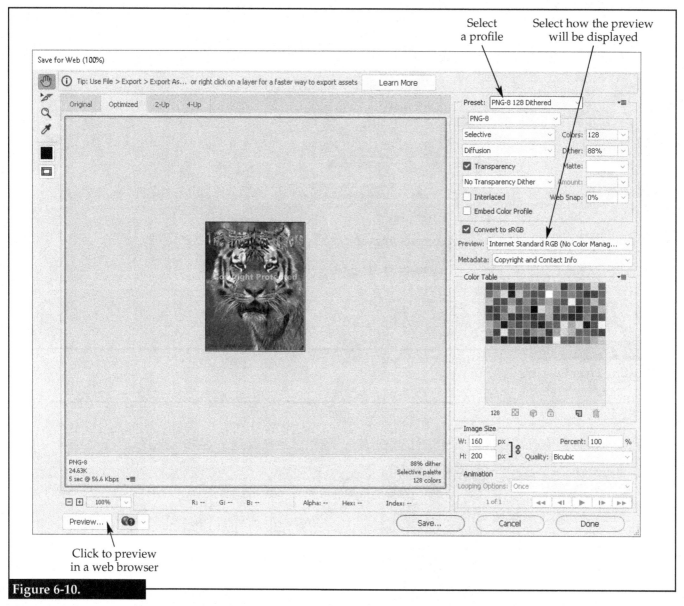

Select a profile

Select how the preview will be displayed

Click to preview in a web browser

Figure 6-10.

Saving an image for use on a website.

TIP
Three common image file types used on web pages are PNG, JPEG, and GIF.

93. Click the **Preset:** drop-down arrow, and click **PNG-8 128 Dithered** in the drop-down menu. The settings in the dialog box change to allow a low-quality image using only 128 colors.

94. Click the **Preview:** drop-down arrow, and click **Internet Standard RGB (No Color Management)** in the drop-down list. This setting determines how the image is displayed when previewed in a web browser.

95. Click the **Preview...** button at the bottom-left corner of the dialog box. The image is displayed in the default web browser. Information about the image and some HTML code is also displayed in the browser window.

96. Close the web browser window.

97. Click the **Save...** button. The **Save Optimized As** dialog box is displayed.

98. Click in the **File name:** text box, and enter *LastName*_Tiger_Web Thumb.

99. Click the **Format:** drop-down arrow, and click **Images Only** in the drop-down list.

100. Navigate to your working folder, and click the **Save** button.

101. Click **Save As...** in the **File** pull-down menu. In the **Save As** dialog box, name the file *LastName*_Tiger_Web Thumb 2, and set the file type as PNG. Notice the **As a Copy** check box is automatically selected because saving in this file type must be done as a copy.

102. Navigate to your working folder, and click the **Save** button. In the **PNG Options** dialog box that is displayed, click the **None/Fast** and the **Interlaced** radio buttons, and then click the **OK** button.

Printing and Scaling

There are many options when printing from Photoshop. The image can be scaled to fit the paper size, printed as a proof, or more options.

103. Close the Tiger.psd file without saving the changes, and then reopen the file. By discarding the changes and reopening the file, the last saved state is restored, which is the large-size image.

104. Click **Print...** in the **File** pull-down menu. The **Photoshop Print Settings** dialog box is displayed.

105. In the **Printer Setup** area of the dialog box, click the **Printer:** drop-down arrow, and click the printer to use in the drop-down list.

106. In the **Printer Setup** area, click the **Print paper in landscape orientation** button. Notice the preview changes, and the image is cut off along the top and bottom because the image is taller than 8.5″.

107. Scroll down to the **Position and Size** area, and check the **Scale to Fit Media** check box. Notice the preview changes to show the entire image fitting on the page.

108. Click the **Rendering Intent** drop-down arrow in the **Color Management** area, and click **Relative Colormetric** in the drop-down list. *Relative colormetric* adjusts colors that are out of gamut to the nearest color in gamut. Since the image is being converted from RGB to CMYK, some color adjustment will occur. The RGB color blue = 255 cannot be accurately reproduced by a CMYK printer. Likewise, the CMYK color cyan = 100% cannot be accurately displayed on a computer monitor in RGB.

109. In the **Color Management** area, click the drop-down arrow that is currently set to **Normal Printing**, and click **Hard Proofing** in the drop-down list.

110. Click the **Proof Setup:** drop-down arrow, and click **Working CMYK** in the drop-down list. This tells Photoshop to render RGB color as CMYK color for the printer.

111. Click the **Print** button. The image is output to the selected printer.

112. Close Photoshop without saving changes.

Lesson Review

Vocabulary

In a word processing document or on a sheet of paper, list all of the *key terms* in this lesson. Place each term on a separate line. Then, write a definition for each term using your own words. You will continue to build this terminology dictionary throughout this certification guide.

Review Questions

Answer the following questions. These questions are aligned to questions in the certification exam. Answering these questions will help prepare you to take the exam.

1. Briefly describe how to remove red-eye from a photograph.

_____

2. How can a pixel mask be semitransparent?

_____

_____

3. Briefly describe how to set a brush to paint in the shape of blades of grass.

_____

_____

4. How can a vertical guideline be placed at an exact location on an image?

_____

_____

5. Compare and contrast kerning and tracking.

_____

_____

6. Text has been added on a layer named Writing. Below this layer is a layer named Trees that contains an image of a forest. List the steps needed to make the text on the Writing layer appear to be filled with the image on the Trees layer.

_____

_____

_____

7. What provides worldwide copyright protection for intellectual property?

_____

8. What is a watermark?

_____

_____

9. What is the difference between a picture package and a contact sheet?

_____

_____

10. Define thumbnail image.

_____

11. Describe how to change the resolution of an image from 72 pixels per inch to 300 pixels per inch without changing the inch dimensions.

_____

_____

12. When changing the size of an image, how is the aspect ratio kept the same?

   _____

   _____

13. A designer has created an image that is 200 pixels wide and 300 pixels high. The image is scaled up so it is larger and now is 600 pixels wide. If the aspect ratio is unchanged, what is the new image height in pixels?

   _____

14. If an image is currently 3″ wide by 2″ high at 600 dpi, what would be the resulting image size in inches if the resolution is changed to 150 dpi?

   _____

15. Which saving command automates the process of saving an image for use on a web page?

   _____

16. List three common file formats used for images on web pages.

   _____

17. How can an image that is larger than the paper size be fully printed on the paper?

   _____

   _____

18. Summarize what the **Working CMYK** option does when printing a hard proof.

   _____

   _____

Lesson 7
Compositing Images

Objectives

Students will create a composite image. Students will explain the process of exporting a layer as an image file. Students will describe how to modify existing image pixels. Students will perform a free transformation.

Situation

The Nocturnal Interactive Computer Entertainment (NICE) wants a photo-based image of the superhero. Your task is to build on the work you completed earlier to finalize the photo-based image. You will composite the images of the face and the tiger to create the final image.

How to Begin

1. Launch Photoshop.
2. Open the *LastName*_TigerMan_1 file from earlier.
3. Organize the layers so the Tiger layer is above the Face Isolated layer, and turn on the visibility of the Face Isolated layer.

Creating a Composite Image

A composite image consists of two or more images. There are several types of composite images, but one of the most common is to blend two images.

4. With the Tiger layer selected, click in the **Opacity:** text box in the **Layers** panel, and enter 40%. Notice how the face is showing through the tiger. This is a basic composited image, but can be made to look much better.
5. Make sure the Tiger layer is selected, and click **Transform** and then **Scale** in the **Edit** pull-down menu. The scaling tool will allow you to change the size of the tiger to better match the face.
6. Drag the top and bottom handles as needed so the important facial landmarks of the nose and the chin on both the face and the tiger are at the same vertical level. *Landmarks* are critical features on an image. Do not worry about the eyes landmark yet. Zoom in and out as needed while scaling the image.
7. Press the [Enter] key to accept the scaling change.
8. With the Tiger layer selected, click **Transform** and then **Warp** in the **Edit** pull-down menu. A cage, or gizmo, is added around the image, as shown in **Figure 7-1.** By bending the cage, the layer can be stretched and squashed, or warped, until the eyes are in position. The vertical and horizontal lines of the cage help keep the alignment correct.
9. Use the handles to stretch the cage so the eyes line up while keeping the chin and nose properly placed. This will take some time and you will likely need to make many adjustments.
10. Adjust the cage so the ears of the tiger are inside the man's hair. Later, when the layers are reordered, the man's hair will cover up the tiger's ears.
11. Press [Enter] to accept the warping change. If you are not happy with the result, undo the operation and start over.
12. Applying what you have learned, set the opacity of the Tiger layer to 100%.
13. Applying what you have learned, display the **Load Selection** dialog box and specify the Face Selection.
14. Check the **Invert** check box in the **Load Selection** dialog box. This setting has the same effect as loading the selection and then inverting the selection. Click the **OK** button to load the inverted selection.
15. Applying what you have learned, remove the areas of the Tiger layer outside of the face. Then, deselect the area.

Exporting a Layer

A single layer or multiple layers of a composite image can be exported to a new file. There are two ways in which to do this: the **Export As...** command and the **Quick Export As PNG** command.

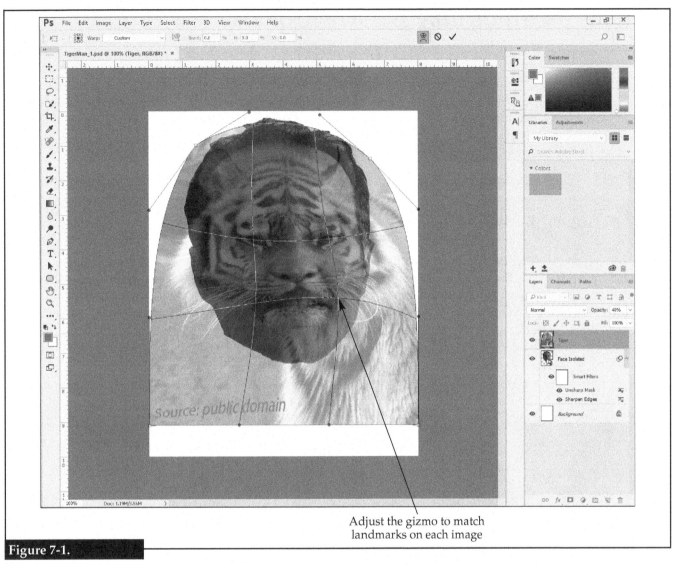

Adjust the gizmo to match
landmarks on each image

Figure 7-1.

Using a gizmo to warp the image.

16. Right-click on the Tiger layer in the **Layers** panel. Notice the **Export As...** and **Quick Export As PNG** commands are available in the shortcut menu.

17. Click the **Layer** pull-down menu. Notice the commands are also available in this menu.

18. Click **Export As...** in the pull-down menu. The **Export As** dialog box is displayed. There are many options for fine-tuning the new file, including selecting the file format. Click the **Cancel** button to close the dialog box without saving the file.

19. Select the **Quick Export As PNG** command, either in the pull-down menu or the shortcut menu in the **Layers** panel. A standard **Save As** dialog box is displayed. There are no options to set when using this command.

20. Navigate to your working folder, and save the layer as a PNG file named Distorted Tiger. Notice the original file remains open. The layer is saved in a separate file, and can be opened and edited if needed.

TIP

When using the **Quick Export As PNG** command, the file type is always PNG. Even if you enter a different file extension, Photoshop saves the file as a PNG file and includes the .png extension.

Modifying Existing Pixels

Photoshop has many uses. It can be used to sharpen, crop, clean up, and otherwise modify a photograph. However, it can also be used to create new parts of an image from scratch. An entire image can also be created from scratch. One technique used for this is to modify existing pixels with commands such as the **Blur Tool** and **Smudge Tool**.

21. Applying what you have learned, move the Face Isolated layer to the top of the layer stack.

22. Applying what you have learned, add a layer mask to the Face Isolated layer, and set the foreground color to medium gray (such as R150, G150, B150).

23. Applying what you have learned, select the Soft Round brush and set its diameter to 25 pixels.

24. Use the brush to paint in the tiger image around the face, as shown in **Figure 7-2.** Do *not* brush over the eyes, mouth, ears, or hair. Turning off the visibility of the Tiger layer can help better display the mask. If needed, change the brush or size to clean up the eyes and mouth. Zoom and pan as needed.

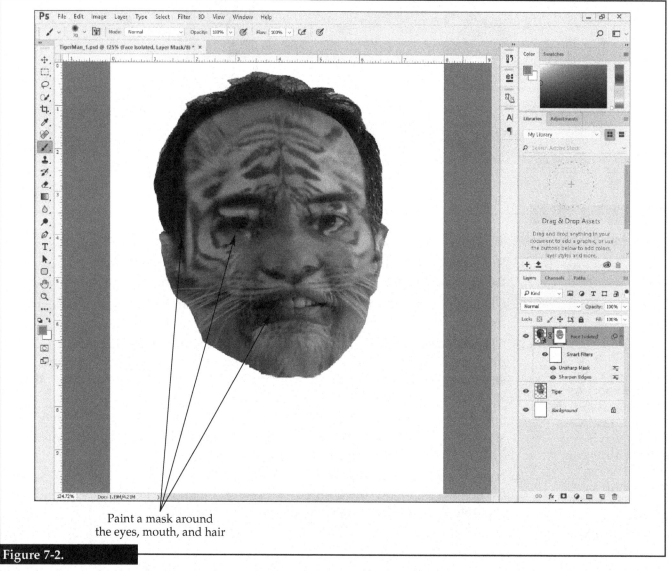

Paint a mask around the eyes, mouth, and hair

Figure 7-2.

Painting a mask onto the layer.

25. Applying what you have learned, flatten the layers.

26. Right-click on the background layer in the **Layers** panel, and click **Duplicate Layer...** in the shortcut menu. In the **Duplicate Layer** dialog box that is displayed, click in the **As:** text box, enter Tiger Man, and click the **OK** button. This makes an exact copy of the layer.

27. Applying what you have learned, rasterize the Tiger Man layer, if it is not already a raster layer.

28. Right-click on the background layer in the **Layers** panel, and click **Delete Layer** in the shortcut menu. When prompted, click the **Yes** button to delete the layer.

Blur Tool

29. Click the **Blur Tool** button in the **Tools** panel. Click and drag around the bottom edge of the face to blur the image by interpolating pixels where the tool is dragged. The hard edge of the face is too crisp for fur, and this will soften the edge. You may need to make a couple of passes.

Smudge Tool

30. Click the **Smudge Tool** in the **Tools** panel. Click on the bottom edge of the face, and drag downward. This will provide the illusion of fur sticking out, as shown in **Figure 7-3.** Repeat this as needed.

31. Save the file as *LastName*_TigerMan_2 in your working folder.

Free Transformations

The **Polygonal Lasso Tool** is helpful in selecting parts of an image that are regular geometric shapes such as the image inside a frame , but can be used to select an irregular geometric shape. Each time you click with the polygonal lasso tool, it places a node. When you move from a node, a line is drawn. The shape must end at the starting node. You will use this tool along with a free transformation to create fangs for the tiger man. A *free transformation* is an operation in which you can scale, rotate, skew, distort, change perspective, or warp the image.

Polygonal Lasso Tool

32. Click the **Polygonal Lasso Tool** button in the **Tools** panel.

33. Applying what you have learned, zoom in on the mouth.

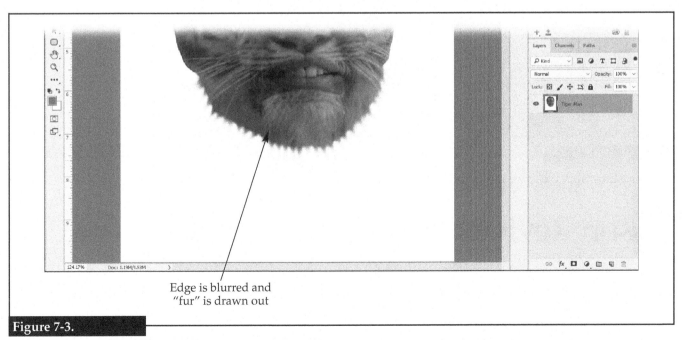

Edge is blurred and "fur" is drawn out

Figure 7-3.

The **Blur Tool** can be used to create fur along the edge.

34. Click once where the left-hand front tooth (on the right in the image) meets the upper lip to place the first node.

35. Click around the tooth to approximate the outline. Click the first node to complete the selection,

36. Press the [Ctrl][C] key combination to copy the selection, then press the [Ctrl][V] key combination to paste it as a new layer.

37. Rename the new layer as Left Fang.

TIP
A free transformation can also be achieved by clicking **Free Transform** in the **Edit** pull-down menu.

38. Applying what you have learned, move the pasted tooth to the right in the image so it is in the corner of the mouth.

39. With the **Move Tool** active, click to select **Show Transform Controls** in the **Options** bar. A transform gizmo is placed around the image on the layer to allow for free transformation.

40. Drag the bottom handle down to elongate the tooth.

41. Hold the [Ctrl] key, click one of the bottom-corner handles, and drag inward to make the tooth pointed so it looks like a fang, as shown in **Figure 7-4.**

42. Press the [Enter] key to set the transformation.

43. Applying what you have learned, create the another fang on the opposite side of the mouth.

44. Save the file, and close Photoshop.

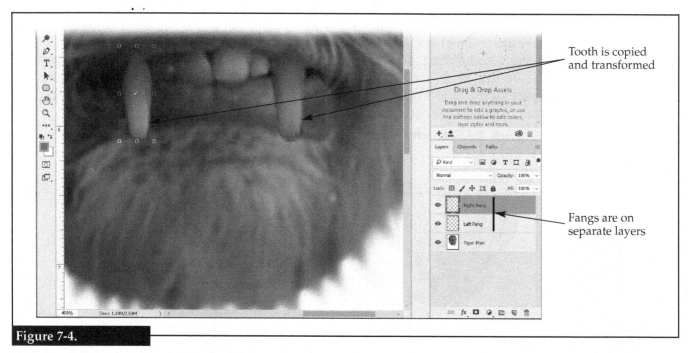

Figure 7-4.

Creating fangs from a copied tooth.

Lesson Review

Vocabulary

In a word processing document or on a sheet of paper, list all of the *key terms* in this lesson. Place each term on a separate line. Then, write a definition for each term using your own words. You will continue to build this terminology dictionary throughout this certification guide.

Review Questions

Answer the following questions. These questions are aligned to questions in the certification exam. Answering these questions will help prepare you to take the exam.

1. Describe the purpose of the **Warp** tool.

_____

_____

2. Which two commands can be used to save a layer as a separate image file?

_____

3. Describe how to load the inverse of a saved selection.

_____

_____

4. What is the purpose of the **Blur Tool**?

_____

_____

5. How does the **Polygonal Lasso Tool** function?

_____

_____

Lesson 8
Outputting Client Changes

Objectives

Students will convert an image to grayscale. Students will set the foreground and background colors. Students will balance color saturation. Students will apply layer styles to text. Students will change the canvas size. Students will create a new layer style. Students will replace a selected color with a new color. Students will adjust image contrast. Students will add metadata to an image.

Situation

The Nocturnal Interactive Computer Entertainment (NICE) company has sent the client soft proofs of the superhero images you created. The client has suggested changes to the image before using it. Complete the changes and create the required output proofs.

How to Begin

1. Launch Photoshop.

2. Open the *LastName*_TigerMan_2 file created in the last lesson.

3. Applying what you have learned, flatten the image, select the background, and save the selection as TigerMan. Deselect the active selection.

Converting to Grayscale

The client has requested a photograph in black and white. This version will be used in a newspaper print advertisement. A black-and-white image is called a *grayscale* image. All pixels are converted to black, white, or a shade of gray.

4. Click **Adjustments** and then **Black & White...** in the **Image** pull-down menu. The **Black and White** dialog box is displayed, as shown in **Figure 8-1**.

5. Click the **OK** button to accept all default settings. The image is converted to grayscale.

6. Save the file in your working folder as a JPEG-format file named *LastName*_TigerMan_B-W. In the **JPEG Options** dialog box, click the **OK** button to accept the defaults.

Adjust the influence of colors

Figure 8-1.
Converting an image to grayscale.

Setting Foreground and Background Color

The client wants a solid fill layer behind the tiger man image. The color selected by the client to use for the background is yellow.

7. Applying what you have learned, undo the color conversion.

8. Double-click the background layer in the **Layers** panel. The **New Layer** dialog box is displayed. Name the layer TigerMan.

9. Click the **Set foreground color** swatch on **Tools** panel. A color picker is displayed.

10. Change the color to R255, G255, and B0. Close the color picker.

11. Click the **Set background color** swatch on **Tools** panel, and change the color to pure blue (R0, G0, B255).

12. Applying what you have learned, create a new solid fill layer named Backdrop Fill. Do not select a color, which forces Photoshop to use the current foreground color.

13. Drag the Backdrop Fill layer below the TigerMan layer in the layer stack.

14. Click the **Eyedropper Tool** button on the **Tools** panel, and click an orange area of the tiger's fur. The tool sets the foreground color to the sampled color.

Eyedropper Tool

Paint Bucket Tool

15. Click the **Paint Bucket Tool** button on the tools panel, and click anywhere on the Backdrop Fill layer. A message appears asking if you want to rasterize the layer. Click the **Yes** button.

16. Click anywhere on the Backdrop Layer. The color you click is replaced with the new foreground color. In this case, since the entire layer was yellow, the entire layer is replaced with the new orange foreground color. The TigerMan layer currently hides the Backdrop Fill layer, but the thumbnail in the **Layers** panel reflects the change to orange.

17. Applying what you have learned, load the TigerMan selection, and delete the white background on the TigerMan layer.

18. Save the file in your working folder as a JPEG-format file named *LastName_Tigerman_Color.*

Select the channel   Adjust the saturation

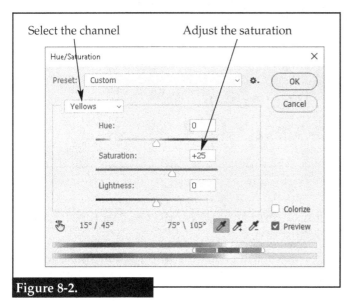

Figure 8-2.

Adjusting the saturation of only the yellows.

Balancing Color Saturation

The client feels the tiger effect is not pronounced enough and would like it to be more orange-yellow. To correct this, you need to balance the colors in the image to increase the amount of yellow.

19. Make the TigerMan layer active, and deselect any active selection.

20. Click **Adjustments** and then **Hue/Saturation...** in the **Image** pull-down menu. The **Hue/Saturation** dialog box is displayed, as shown in **Figure 8-2.**

21. Click the drop-down arrow currently set to **Master**, and click **Yellows** in the drop-down list.

22. Click in the **Saturation:** text box, and enter +25.

23. Click the **OK** button to close the dialog box and apply the setting.

Applying Layer Styles to Text

Antialiasing is used when an image has an alias effect. *Antialiasing* blends the edges of an image or element, such as text, by averaging foreground and background colors. This will smooth the edge to make it look less jagged. Additionally, antialiasing is applied to remove a moiré effect. *Moiré* is an unwanted irregular or wavy pattern in an image, as shown in **Figure 8-3.** This typically occurs on fabric, bricks, and other objects that have vertical and horizontal line patterns. This can also occur when reducing a digital image. If the pixels are compressed, eliminated, or overlap, moiré can occur. In addition to using antialiasing, an unsharp mask can be applied to reduce the sharpness of lines or moiré.

24. Applying what you have learned, add horizontal text in sans serif typeface that states Tiger Man, and place it below the face. Set the color to red and the size to 60.

25. With the text layer active, click the **Add a layer style** button in the **Layers** panel and click **Drop Shadow...** in the drop-down menu. The **Layer Style** dialog box is displayed with **Drop Shadow** automatically selected. A *drop shadow* is a

Add a Layer Style

Moiré

Figure 8-3.

Moiré is an unwanted irregular or wavy pattern in an image.

shadow behind a layer or selection. A drop shadow is offset to cast the shadow in the opposite direction of the light source.

26. Click in the **Angle:** text box, enter to −45, and check the **Use Global Light** check box. This sets the light source as a global light similar to the sun at −45 degrees from the zero position, which is the right side of the circle. Notice in the preview and in the image the shadow is cast opposite of the angle. This is just like in real life if you shine a flashlight on an object, the shadow would be opposite of the position of the flashlight.

27. Drag the **Distance:**, **Spread:**, and **Size:** sliders to see how each setting changes the effect.

28. Click the **Contour:** drop-down arrow. A drop-down menu is displayed containing options for setting how the effect is applied. Click each one to see the differences, then select a contour shape of your choice.

29. Check the **Anti-aliased** check box. Depending on which contour style you selected, the effect may be very subtle.

30. Click in the **Noise:** text box, and enter 30%. *Noise* is the term for a random pattern that is used to give digital images a more natural look. Noise creates flaws in the image to break up straight lines and solid fills.

31. Click the **OK** button to apply the effect, as shown in **Figure 8-4.** Notice the icon next to the layer name in the **Layers** panel that indicates a layer style has been applied.

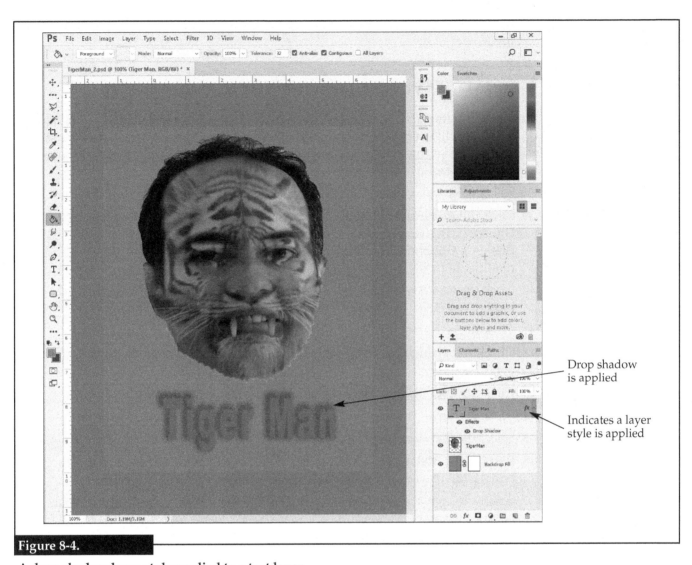

Drop shadow is applied

Indicates a layer style is applied

Figure 8-4.

A drop shadow layer style applied to a text layer.

Increasing the Canvas Size

The client wants this image to appear as a full-page illustration in a printed book. Have you noticed how it is hard to read the text of a book that is closest to the binding? This area is called the *gutter.* To compensate for the gutter, the canvas size of the image needs to be expanded to one side so the image is not hidden in the gutter. The image will appear on a left-hand page, and the printer specifications call for a five pica gutter for all images. This means the canvas needs to be expanded by five picas on the right-hand side. On a left-hand page, the gutter is on the right.

32. Applying what you have learned, open the **Canvas Size** dialog box.

33. Change the units of measurement to picas.

34. Add five picas to the current width dimension.

35. Select the correct anchor point so the canvas will be expanded only to the right-hand side.

36. Apply the change. Notice the fill layer does not automatically expand to fit the new canvas size. The gray and white checkerboard pattern visible on the right-hand side of the canvas indicates a transparent background.

37. Applying what you have learned, add the orange color to the white area of the fill layer.

Creating New Layer Styles

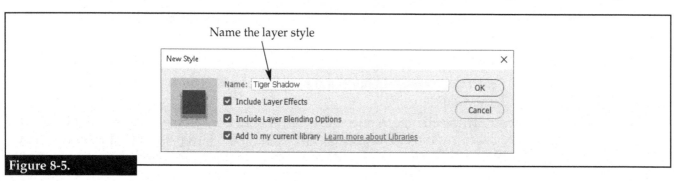

The client wants the drop shadow on the text to be exactly duplicated on the face. To do this, you will need to copy the style used on the text layer or create a new style with the same settings. In this case, creating a new style will make it easier to apply the drop shadow to other objects added to this image.

Add a Layer Style

38. Select the text layer.

39. Click the **Add a layer style** button in the **Layers** panel and click **Blending Options...** in the drop-down menu. The **Layer Style** dialog box is displayed with **Blending Options** automatically selected, which shows all style options and modifications for this layer.

40. Click the **New Style...** button. The **New Style** dialog box is displayed, as shown in **Figure 8-5.**

41. Click in the **Name:** text box, and enter Tiger Shadow.

42. Check the **Include Layer Effects** and **Include Layer Blending Options** check boxes.

43. Click the **OK** button to save the new layer style.

44. Close the **Layer Style** dialog box.

45. Select the TigerMan layer.

46. Display the **Styles** panel by clicking **Window>Styles** on the **Menu** bar. The **Styles** panel is displayed in the **Libraries** panel group and made active.

47. Scroll through the image tiles, and click the image tile for the Tiger Shadow style. Notice the same style of drop shadow applied to the text is applied to the face.

48. Applying what you have learned, assign the Sun Faded Photo style to the fill layer.

49. Save the file in your working folder as a TIFF-format file named *LastName_* TigerMan_Book. In the **TIFF Options** dialog box, click the **None** radio button, and then click the **OK** button. When prompted regarding layers, click the **OK** button to include layers.

TIP

A new style based on the settings of the current layer can be created by clicking the **Create new style** button in the **Styles** panel.

Replacing Color

The client has some additional requirements for the image. The specifications call for the tiger man to be based on blue tones instead of orange tones. The output

Name the layer style

New Style	×

Name: Tiger Shadow ☑ Include Layer Effects ☑ Include Layer Blending Options ☑ Add to my current library Learn more about Libraries

OK

Cancel

Figure 8-5.

Creating a new layer style.

must be in a format that a different digital designer can use to complete the design, so the client as requested the image be in RAW format. *RAW format* keeps all of the photograph and editing information without rasterization or compression. This format is an uncompressed bitmap file and can be used by almost any photo-editing software. It is common file format produced by digital cameras.

50. Select the TigerMan layer.

51. Click **Adjustments** and then **Replace Color...** in the **Image** pull-down menu. The **Replace Color** dialog box is displayed, as shown in **Figure 8-6.** Notice the default color is the same as the current foreground color.

52. Click the **Image** radio button and make sure the **Preview** check box is checked to show the image in the preview.

53. Click the **Eyedropper Tool** button in the dialog box, and then click on an orange part of the image. This can be done in the preview or in the canvas area.

54. Click in the **Fuzziness:** text box, and enter 125. This will affect a more diffused spread of colors analogous to the selected color.

55. Drag the **Hue:** slider until the **Result** preview tile displays blue.

56. Drag the **Saturation:** slider to create a bright blue.

57. Click the **OK** button to replace the orange with blue.

58. Save the file in your working folder as a RAW-format file named *LastName_* TigerMan_Blue. In the **Photoshop RAW Options** dialog box, click the **OK** button to accept the default settings.

59. Click **Print Size** in the **View** pull-down menu. This displays a zoom level that shows the image in the size as it will print.

60. Save the file in your working folder as a PSD-format file named *LastName_* TigerMan_Blue.

TIP
Click the **Selection** radio button in the **Replace Color** dialog box to see the selection mask.

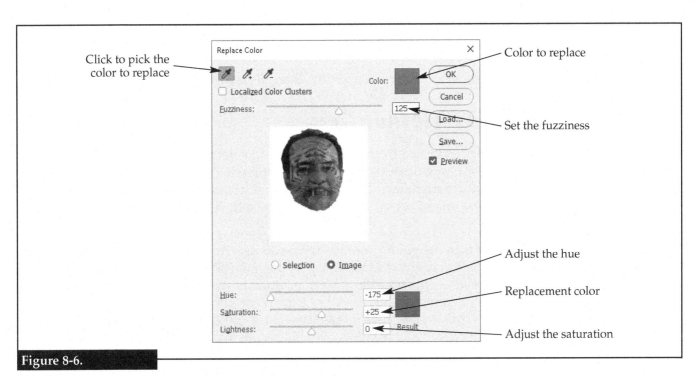

Figure 8-6.

Replacing a specific color in the image with a new color.

Adjusting Contrast

The client reported that the blue face does not show up good enough against the background. Additionally, the white fur needs to be more dominant and less blurry. Follow the steps below to change the image contrast.

61. Select the TigerMan layer.

62. Click **Auto Color** in the **Image** pull-down menu. Photoshop automatically adjusts the color balance and all the color point levels, including black and white.

63. Click **Auto Contrast** in the **Image** pull-down menu. Photoshop automatically adjusts the levels of adjoining colors.

64. Applying what you have learned, undo the last two operations. You will manually adjust the color and contrast to have more control.

65. Click **Adjustments** and then **Brightness/Contrast...** in the **Image** pull-down menu. The **Brightness/Contrast** dialog box is displayed.

66. Click in the **Brightness:** text box, and enter 30. This will lighten the image.

67. Click in the **Contrast:** text box, and enter 50. This will enhance the blue and bring up more white, which will make the white fur be a bit more dominant.

68. Click the **OK** button to apply the changes. The image still needs a little adjusting to get back the quality.

69. Click **Auto Tone** in the **Image** pull-down menu. The overall tonal value of the image is adjusted.

Dodge Tool

70. Click the **Dodge Tool** button in the **Tools** panel. *Dodging* is a process that lightens an area of the image.

71. Applying what you have learned, set the brush to Soft Round with a size of 45.

72. Paint over darker areas of the image to make them lighter.

73. Click the **Burn Tool** button in the **Tools** panel. *Burning* is a process that darkens an area of the image.

Burn Tool

74. Paint over lighter areas of the image to make them darker.

Sponge Tool

75. Click the **Sponge Tool** button in the **Tools** panel. The **Sponge Tool** soaks up color like a sponge soaks up water. It removes color from an area of the image.

76. Paint around the mouth and anywhere else where blue should be removed.

Adding Metadata

It is an important step in any project to include metadata. *Metadata* provide information about other data, such as a document. On an image, metadata may include the artist's name, company, and copyright information. This will help identify any unauthorized uses of the image and alert people to the original creator of the work.

Work that is in the *public domain* has no owner. Anybody can use it or do anything to it. Even a copyrighted work can enter the public domain. An old book, painting, song, or other work will enter the public domain when the copyright has expired and is not or cannot be renewed. For example, you can reprint Shakespeare plays without permission as these works have entered the public domain. However, you cannot reprint a new book about Shakespeare plays because that book is copyrighted.

In some limited situations, copyrighted materials can be used without permission as governed by fair use doctrine. Under *fair use doctrine,* copyrighted material can be reprinted or displayed for the purpose of describing or reviewing the creative work, such as a student doing a report or a movie critic providing a review. The person using the copyrighted materials is describing or commenting on the work, not claiming ownership of it.

Designers must take extra care when using photographs of people. If the photograph contains a recognizable person, the photographer should have a model release signed by that person. A *model release* is a liability-waiver document that states the person in the image grants the photographer certain rights to the use of the photograph. Most public images of celebrities, politicians, and public figures do not require a model release when used in compliance with the Freedom of Speech right of the country in which the photograph is used. However, commercial uses of such photographs, for example the promotion of a product that implies an endorsement, are usually considered an infringement on the person's rights. The best practice to avoid liabilities is to obtain a model release whenever using a photograph of an identifiable person regardless whether the person is a public figure or not.

77. Click **File Info...** in the **File** pull-down menu. A dialog box is displayed in which metadata can be entered, as shown in **Figure 8-7.** Click the **Basic** category.

78. Enter Tiger Man in the **Document Title:** text box, your name in the **Author:** text box, and Artist in the **Author Title:** text box.

79. Click the middle star to give the image a three-star rating.

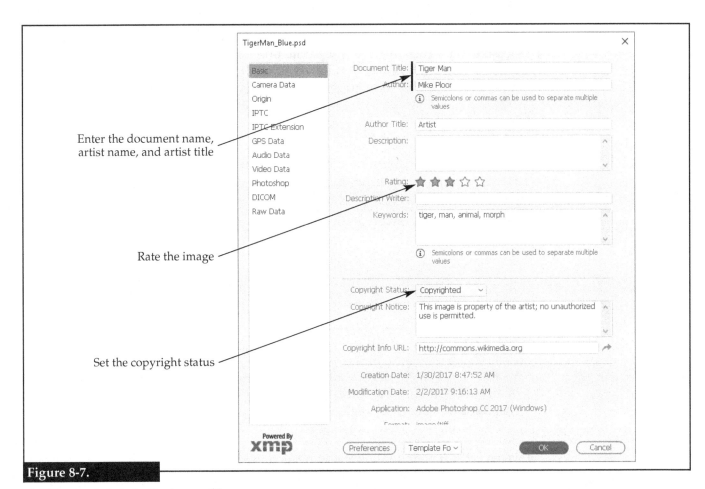

Figure 8-7.

Adding metadata to the image file.

80. Click in the **Keywords:** text box, and enter tiger, man, animal, morph. These are terms used in keyword searches.

81. Click the **Copyright Status:** drop-down arrow, and click **Copyrighted** in the drop-down menu. Do *not* click **Public Domain** unless you have no desire to keep the copyright on the image.

82. Click in the **Copyright Notice:** text box, and enter This image is property of the artist; no unauthorized use is permitted.

83. Click in the **Copyright Info URL:** text box, and enter http://commons.wikimedia.org. Wikimedia is one of many free image-storage locations that apply a standard license to the image. The artist need not be a lawyer to apply a license to the image. By selecting a few options, the artist can specify how the image can be used by others. Options such as author attributed, image use, edits allowable, and many more can be applied to customize the license.

84. Click the **OK** button to add the metadata to the image file.

85. Save the file in your working folder as a PSD-format file named *LastName_TigerMan_Final*.

86. Close Photoshop.

Lesson Review

Vocabulary

In a word processing document or on a sheet of paper, list all of the *key terms* in this lesson. Place each term on a separate line. Then, write a definition for each term using your own words. You will continue to build this terminology dictionary throughout this certification guide.

Review Questions

Answer the following questions. These questions are aligned to questions in the certification exam. Answering these questions will help prepare you to take the exam.

1. Describe how to convert an image to black and white (grayscale).

_____

_____

_____

2. What color is the default color for a new solid fill layer?

_____

3. Which tools are used to select an exact color from a photograph and to flood that color into another area?

_____

4. What is the path to the command needed to change saturation of only the yellows?

_____

5. What does antialiasing do?

_____

_____

6. What is moiré?

_____

_____

7. Describe how to create a new style from a selected text layer.

_____

_____

_____

_____

8. What is the path to the command needed to replace the color and change the hue?

_____

9. Which view is best to preview the image in the same size that it will print?

_____

10. Which command tells Photoshop to automatically adjust color levels?

_____

11. Which tool is used to darken an area?

_____

12. If taking a photograph of a person to be used in an advertisement, what should the photographer obtain from the person?

_____

13. What are metadata?

_____

_____

14. What copyright protection do you have if you mark the image as public domain?

_____

15. Summarize how a screen shot of a copyrighted video game character could be used under the fair use doctrine.

_____

_____

_____

_____

Answers

Lesson 1

1. Shape, form, line, color, value, space, and texture.
2. Regular shapes and objects that are used to assemble more complex shapes or objects.
3. The primary colors of red, blue, and yellow.
4. A complementary color is located opposite of the selected color on the color wheel, while an analogous color is located next to the selected color.
5. Positive space is the area or volume occupied by the primary objects, while negative space is the area or volume around or between the primary objects.
6. The point or points in a perspective drawing where receding parallel lines appear to meet.
7. Movement, emphasis, harmony, variety, balance, contrast, proportion, pattern, and unity.
8. Movement.
9. Emphasis.
10. Balance.
11. An image is divided into three sections horizontally and three sections vertically to create nine areas, and where the lines cross are the focal points for a scene.
12. Contrast.
13. Unity.
14. To achieve site-wide consistency.
15. Shorter development time, easier maintenance, and improved usability.

Lesson 2

1. PNG-24
2. GIF, PNG-8, PNG-24, JPEG, BMP, and RAW or CIFF. (There are other file types.)
3. CGM, AI, and EPS. (There are other file types.)
4. RGB color model at a resolution of 72 or 96 dpi.
5. The alpha channel allows for a masking color, which is a single shade of a color that determines areas of transparency in the image.
6. Vector.
7. The process of converting a raster image into a vector image.
8. Raster images are composed of colored dots at specified locations, while vector images are composed of elements recorded by their mathematical definitions.
9. Applying the most appropriate resolution and file compression.
10. Bitmap is device-independent and SVG is supported by most browsers and mobile devices.
11. L*A*B color works for both video displays (RGB) and printed materials (CMYK).
12. 10.1" ($728 \div 72 = 10.1$) × 1.25" ($90 \div 72 = 1.25$)
13. Bicubic for enlargement.
14. A serif font has decorations called serifs at the ends of letters, while a sans serif font lacks these decorations.
15. Sans serif.

Copyright Goodheart-Willcox Co., Inc.

Lesson 3

Figure 3-3

1. Move Tool
2. Rectangular Marquee Tool
3. Lasso Tool
4. Quick Selection Tool
5. Crop Tool
6. Eyedropper Tool
7. Spot Healing Brush Tool
8. Edit in Quick Mask Mode
9. Magic Wand Tool
10. Healing Brush Tool
11. Art History Brush Tool
12. Sharpen Tool
13. Burn Tool
14. Rotate View Tool
15. Magnetic Lasso Tool
16. Slice Tool
17. Color Sampler Tool
18. Patch Tool
19. Color Replacement Tool
20. Content-Aware Move Tool
21. Vertical Type Mask Tool
22. Note Tool
23. Convert Point Tool
24. Pencil Tool
25. Clone Stamp Tool
26. History Brush Tool
27. Eraser Tool
28. Gradient Tool
29. Blur Tool
30. Dodge Tool
31. Change Screen Mode
32. Perspective Crop Tool
33. Brush Tool
34. Background Eraser Tool
35. Pen Tool
36. Vertical Type Tool
37. Magic Eraser Tool
38. Material Drop Tool
39. Smudge Tool
40. Sponge Tool
41. Add Anchor Point Tool
42. Mixer Brush Tool
43. Polygon Tool
44. Red Eye Tool
45. Custom Shape Tool
46. Pen Tool
47. Horizontal Type Tool
48. Path Selection Tool
49. Zoom Tool
50. Elliptical Marquee Tool
51. Polygonal Lasso Tool
52. Material Eyedropper Tool
53. Pattern Stamp Tool
54. Paint Bucket Tool
55. Direct Selection Tool
56. Rounded Rectangle Tool
57. Single Row Marquee Tool
58. Horizontal Type Mask Tool
59. Ellipse Tool
60. Single Column Marquee Tool
61. Slice Select Tool
62. Ruler Tool
63. Delete Anchor Point Tool
64. Count Tool

Review Questions

1. Sample graphics and the final image.
2. Conduct preproduction interviews.
3. Client goals set the direction of the creative work, while the target market is the group the people for whom the work is intended.
4. Contact the client and discuss your concerns and possible solutions.
5. Sketches, mockups, and specifications.
6. The image should be linked because it will automatically update when the image is edited and saved in Photoshop.
7. Cultural differences between America and the target market.
8. Light is passed over an image, and the scanner digitally records each point of color.
9. It is approval from the client to create the final output needed.
10. The ability to quickly make changes and cost saving.
11. The **Menu** bar.
12. In the **Options** bar.
13. Collapsed panels have been minimized to icons, while expanded panels have commands visible.
14. Canvas.
15. By the small triangle in the lower-right corner of the button.
16. The outline.
17. The **Color** panel.
18. The **Adjustments** panel.

19. The **Styles** panel.
20. Activate the **Crop Tool**, click the **Straighten** button on the **Options** bar, and click and drag on the image to tell Photoshop what should be horizontal.
21. Click **View>Fit to Screen** on the **Menu** bar.
22. Extend.

23. Move.
24. **Add to Selection**.
25. The vector mask is resolution-independent and has clean edges, while a layer mask is resolution-dependent and uses a bitmap (raster) masking object.

Lesson 4

1. By selecting the left-middle button in the **Anchor:** area of the **Canvas Size** dialog box.
2. Right-click on the selection and click **Select Inverse** in the shortcut menu, and click **Inverse** in the **Select** pull-down menu.
3. Click **Cut** in the **Edit** pull-down menu or press the [Delete] key.
4. It cuts the current selection, creates a new layer, and pastes the selection on the new layer.
5. At the bottom of the **Layers** panel.
6. Stroke.
7. Select the layer in the **Layers** panel, drag it below the other layer, and drop.
8. In the **Layers** panel, double-click on the layer containing the shape, and select a new color in the color picker that is displayed.
9. Click the **Horizontal Type Tool** button, click the location on the canvas where the text is to be placed, and enter the text. The layer is automatically created.
10. The shape is defined by each pixel, and the shape color can no longer be edited by double-clicking the layer.

11. The **Magic Wand Tool**.
12. 1. Create the selection. 2. Click the **Gradient Tool** button. 3. Click the **Linear Gradient** button. 4. Click the Foreground to Background style. 5. Click in the selection and drag to draw the gradient line.
13. At the bottom of the **Layers** panel.
14. Click the workspace switcher, click **New Workspace...** in the drop-down menu, and name the workspace in the **New Workspace** dialog box.
15. **Quick Select Tool**
16. Click **Image>Image Rotation>90° Clockwise** on the **Menu** bar.
17. The text is expanded to exactly end at the left- and right-hand margins, and the last line is aligned to the right.
18. Increase the **Tolerance:** setting on the **Options** bar.
19. The **Snapshot** function in the **History** panel.
20. To display the rulers, click **View>Rulers** on the **Menu** bar. To change the units, right-click on either ruler, and select the new units in the shortcut menu.

Lesson 5

1. The **Magnetic Lasso Tool**.
2. It is loaded by clicking **Load Selection...** in the **Select** pull-down menu.
3. The **Add layer mask** button is located in the **Layers** panel.
4. Nondestructive editing involves making changes that do not permanently eliminate the original image data, while destructive editing eliminates the data.

5. In the settings information display located in the lower-left corner of the screen.
6. All of its layers are collapsed into the background. All visible layers are flattened into a single layer. The file size is reduced. All hidden layers can be deleted if you so choose.
7. Click **Smart Objects** and then **Convert to Smart Object** in the **Layer** pull-down menu, and click **Convert for Smart Filters** in the **Filter** pull-down menu.

8. Any filter is applied as a smart filter if the layer to which it is applied is a smart object.

9. So any filters applied to it are smart filters and can be altered later.

Lesson 6

1. Use the **Red Eye Tool**, and drag a rectangle over the area containing red-eye.

2. By painting with gray instead of white or black.

3. Select the **Brush Tool**, and click the **Brush Preset Picker** drop-down arrow on the **Options** bar and choose the brush with the grass shape.

4. Click **New Guide...** in the **View** pull-down menu, and in the **New Guide** dialog box specify the location of the guideline.

5. Kerning is the spacing between certain letters when they are adjacent to each other, such as A and V, while tracking is the overall spacing between all letters.

6. First, move the Trees layer above the Writing layer in the **Layers** panel, then click the panel menu button in the **Layers** panel, and click **Create Clipping Mask** in the menu.

7. The World Intellectual Property Organization (WIPO) Copyright Treaty.

8. A design or symbol placed on an image to render it unusable, but so that somebody can still view the image.

9. A picture package is a set of multiple copies of a single image fitted onto a single print page,

while a contact sheet contains many different images printed as thumbnail images on a single sheet.

10. It is a small version of the full-size image.

11. Click **Image Size...** in the **Image** pull-down menu, and, in the **Image Size** dialog box, choose a resampling method and enter 300 in the **Resolution:** text box.

12. By checking the **Constrain Proportions** check box in the **Image Size** dialog box to lock the width and height dimensions.

13. 900 pixels (600 pixels new width ÷ 200 pixels previous width = 3 change factor; 300 pixels previous height × 3 change factor = 900 pixels new height)

14. 12″ wide by 8″ high (600 dpi ÷ 150 dpi = 4 change factor; 3″ wide × 4 change factor = 12″ wide; 2″ high × 4 change factor = 8″ high)

15. The **Save for Web...** command in the **File** pull-down menu.

16. PNG, JPEG, and GIF.

17. By checking the **Scale to Fit Media** check box in the **Photoshop Print Settings** dialog box.

18. Photoshop will render RGB color as CMYK color for the printer.

Lesson 7

1. By bending the cage the tool places on the image, the layer can be stretched and squashed, or warped.

2. **Export As...** and **Quick Export As PNG**, both either in the **Layers** pull-down menu or the shortcut menu in the **Layers** panel.

3. Check the **Invert** check box in the **Load Selection** dialog box.

4. It interpolates pixels in the image where the tool is dragged.

5. It is used to create a selection by clicking to draw an irregular or regular geometric shape.

Lesson 8

1. Click **Adjustments** and then **Black & White...** in the **Image** pull-down menu, adjust the color influence in the **Black and White** dialog box, and apply the change.

2. The foreground color.

3. The **Eyedropper Tool** is used to pick up the color, and the **Paint Bucket Tool** is used to apply the color.

4. Click **Adjustments** and then **Hue/Saturation...** in the **Image** pull-down menu.

5. Blends the edges of an image or element, such as text, by averaging foreground and background colors to smooth the edge to make it look less jagged.

6. Unwanted irregular or wavy pattern in an image.

7. Click the **Add a layer style** button in the **Layers** panel and click **Blending Options...** in the drop-down menu, and in the **Layer Style** dialog box click the **New...** button and name the new style.

8. Click **Adjustments** and then **Replace Color...** in the **Image** pull-down menu.

9. Print size.

10. Click **Auto Color** in the **Image** pull-down menu.

11. **Burn Tool.**

12. A model-release form.

13. Information about other data, such as a document; on an image, metadata may include the artist's name, company, and copyright information.

14. Material in the public domain carries no copyright protection.

15. A magazine writer could use the image in a story describing or commenting on the game.